THE BUSY SOUL

*Ten-Minute
Spiritual Workouts
Drawn From
Jewish Tradition*

RABBI TERRY BOOKMAN

A PERIGEE BOOK

Dedicated
to my family and friends
who have been there for me
along every step of this spiritual journey.
You know who you are.

A Perigee Book
Published by The Berkley Publishing Group
A division of Penguin Putnam Inc.
375 Hudson Street
New York, New York 10014

First edition: April 1999

Published simultaneously in Canada.

The Penguin Putnam Inc. World Wide Web site address is
http://www.penguinputnam.com

Library of Congress Cataloging-in-Publication Data

Bookman, Terry.
    The busy soul : ten-minute spiritual workouts drawn from Jewish
tradition / Terry Bookman.—1st ed.
        p.   cm.
    ISBN 0-399-52486-X
    1. Fasts and feasts—Judaism—Meditations.   2. Jewish meditations.
I. Title.
BM690.B553   1999
296.7—dc21   98-32327
                                                                   CIP

Printed in the United States of America

10 9 8 7 6 5 4 3 2

CONTENTS

SUMMER

FALL

ACKNOWLEDGMENTS

My genesis as an author of books came about through a phone call that Marsha Melnick of Round Table Press made to me. She called me one day, having read an article about the Spiritual Check-Ups I was doing with my congregation, at the time, in Milwaukee. Marsha asked, "Have you ever considered writing a book?" And thus began our collaboration.

The idea for *The Busy Soul* was developed through conversations with my friend and agent Julie Merberg. Her insight, energy, and enthusiasm, plus her faith in my work have been an invaluable gift. She is truly an inspiration. We had the concept from the on-line Spiritual Workout I had created due to the urging of another friend, Joe Jacoby. It was he who pushed me to "give the people something accessible" for everyday use. And thus this idea was born. I would love to thank the hundreds of people who utilized the Workout while it was on-line, especially my original "test group." Your feedback and encouragement was invaluable.

My assistant, Claudia Goodman, spent long hours at the computer and telephone with the many versions and recensions of this text. She is a partner, always making me look good. I thank her for her dedication and love.

Working with the people at Putnam/Perigee, especially my editor, Delores McMullen, has been a pleasure and an honor. From the beginning, she has treated me like a valued veteran, not a first-time author. Her intelligence and firm but gentle hand sharpened this text, allowing me to better say what I wanted. I could not have asked for more.

There have been several pioneers in this work of bringing Jewish meditations for daily contemplation. I would like to acknowledge my indebtedness to three of them whose work served as role models for me—Rabbis Bernard Raskas, Kerry Olitzky, and Abraham Twersky.

And lastly, there is my family—Karen Sobel, my life's partner, and our four boys, Ari, Jonah, Micah, and Jesse. They are my rock and my support, putting up with the ridiculous hours I keep to do the work God has called me to do. Words could never thank them. My parents, Arthur and Lillian, and my sister and brother, Frada and Robert, have never failed in their love and support, no matter where my life's journey has taken me. Knowing they were always there for me was often the only faith that sustained me. May God bless them always.

Terry A. Bookman

INTRODUCTION
WHAT IS JEWISH SPIRITUALITY?

A kid on the lam. A mama's boy out in the wilderness, alone, for the very first time in his life. He carries only a satchel with the food his mother prepared for him to take on this journey. Pretending to be Esau before his blind old father, he has stolen his brother's blessing, just as years earlier he tricked him out of his birthright inheritance. Now Jacob is completely alone and there is no turning back.

We can relate to the biblical patriarch Jacob in this state—afraid, alone, imperfect. Jacob was embarking on a journey, with an uncertain destination. We've been there too. Having grown up in the midst of material well-being, having achieved the successes we were meant to achieve, we may still find ourselves in a kind of wilderness, partially inherited, partially of our own making. Where are we? Where are we going? Why are our steps so tenuous? Why does the ground feel so shaky underfoot? We don't know the answers.

Jacob's journey took him from his home in Be'er Sheva toward the old country in Haran. On the first night, he came upon a certain place and stopped to go to sleep. He dreamed a dream of angels ascending and descending on a ladder. At the top of the ladder, there was God. And God said to Jacob, "I am Adonai, the God of Abraham your father and the God of Isaac. This land upon which you are lying I will give to you and your descendants after you. Your descendants shall be as the dust of the earth, spreading out to the four corners of the earth, the west and the east, the north and the south. And all the families of the earth shall bless themselves by you and your descendants. Behold, I am with you. I will guard and watch over you everywhere you go; and I will bring you back to this land, for I will not abandon you until I have done all that I have spoken."

Jacob jumped up out of his sleep. It was still the middle of the night. And he declared, "Surely God is in this place, and I, I did not know it. How awesome is this place! It is none other than the very house of God, and this is the gateway to heaven." And then he went back to bed.

In the morning, Jacob took the stone which had served as his pillow, set it up as a pillar, and anointed it with oil. He renamed the site *Beth El,* House of God, and then he made a vow, saying, "If God remains with me, and watches over me on this journey, giving me bread to eat and clothes to wear, and I return in peace to my father's house, then Adonai will be my God. And this stone that I made into a pillar shall be the site of God's house. And of all that God gives me, I will tithe ten percent."

How would our therapists respond to such an account? Imagine bringing this "dream material" to your regularly scheduled appointment. Your therapist asks, "How did this dream make you feel?" And you say, "Well, it actually made me feel pretty good." And she says, "Well, that makes sense. You were upset. You were frightened. You were alone. You felt guilty about tricking your old, blind father. For all you knew, your tough, buff, athletic, health club brother was chasing you. After all, you had just cheated Esau (for the second time) out of a considerable sum. This dream is self-serving. It assured you that you did the right thing, that God is on your side. So in the morning, cleared of guilt, your confidence restored, you resumed your journey. It makes perfect sense."

Certainly, we can read Jacob's dream as a psychological justification for his crime. But what's more important than the dream is the dreamer's own interpretation. Jacob truly believed God was talking to him in his dream. Rather than seeking vindication for his actions, he was seeking proof of God. This willingness to believe marks the beginning of Jacob's spiritual journey both to himself and to his God, parallel journeys which ultimately lead to the same place. This is the starting point of all our journeys.

We begin by leaving home and everything that is familiar to us. Someday we will return, but the search must start in unfamiliar territory; we are charting new ground. Self-awareness is an ongoing act of discovery. So is God awareness. Steps are taken in small increments, though every once in a while we have a breakthrough experience, in which all is clear and definite. Jacob is an *ish tam,* a kind of naive, soft young man, unknowing, protected, without struggle. Jacob's journey was his "Outward Bound solo"—a test of his survival skills, especially those that come from within.

Do you remember your first real challenge? Was it a relationship that never got realized? Was it going off to college? Or was it your first job? Was it the divorce you thought could never happen to you? The death of someone you loved? Transitions and loss, failures in deed or will, this is the stuff of life that sets us on our journeys, seeking the ladders that will lead us to ourselves and to our God. Every life has such moments of challenge. They weave themselves into the very fabric of who we are and what we can become.

When Jacob woke from his dream in the middle of the night, he was certain of God's presence. For the ancients, the dream world was just another dimension of reality, every bit as real as our conscious, waking existence. Often, it is in dreams that God is revealed and speaks to us because in dreams we are open to hearing what God has to say. The place Jacob thought was any old place turned out to be the House of God, the gateway to heaven. The

Hebrew text uses the word *makom* for "place." *Makom* is also another word for God. The Place. Jacob had really come to God's place, only he did not know it. Was this an unusual place, a holy place? Or was it any old place? The Hebrew allows it to be both.

There are unique places in which we recognize or feel the presence of God. Perhaps we've seen God in a special place in nature like the Grand Canyon, or a favorite spot in our backyard, an altar we have created in our home, or a synagogue. Or maybe we can feel God's presence anyplace, every place we have the awareness and the will to make it so. There are ladders stretching forth from earth to heaven. Angels, busy accompanying us on our journeys, are going up and down, a celestial changing of the guard. God is there as well, at the top of the ladder or at our sides (again, the Hebrew allows for both). Jacob had found God's place without realizing it. Ironically, he had to go to sleep to wake up to this reality. Perhaps we all do.

Every year at the end of the High Holy Day services, something happens. By now, after fifteen years in the rabbinate, I know what to expect. Once the crowd thins out, people come over, sheepish, visibly moved, and they say something like this: "Rabbi, this was the most incredible High Holidays ever. I don't know what it was. But I know things are going to be different for me. I am going to start coming to services more often. I really mean it. I don't want to lose this." And I usually say something like, "Great, I'll look for you next week . . . And if you want to talk some more, just give me a call." They shake my hand or give me a hug, and I don't see them until the following year.

Of course, when I do see them next, I don't bring up their High Holy Day revelation and neither do they. I know it was sincere when they said it. Something happened during services for them. Something genuine. The liturgy struck a chord, an old phrase was heard in a new way, the sermon had particular relevance . . . Or perhaps it was an event in their own lives that made it all look different. A parent had died, a child started dating a non-Jew, business was particularly good . . . They dreamt they felt God's presence.

There are moments in which we are convinced of God's reality, and at these moments we are ready to change our lives. But for most of us, such moments are not enough. We need constant confirmation that what we thought we felt, what we want so desperately to believe in, is real. Even Jacob, who had a very vivid encounter with God that night in the wilderness, awoke with his confidence shaken. We've been there also. You have a dream so convincing you wake up sweating, distressed, elated, convinced that you received some message, some truth. Perhaps, like me, you wrote it down on the pad you keep by your bedside for such a moment. And in the morning, still excited and shaken from your nocturnal experience, you read from the pad and nothing you've jotted down makes sense anymore.

Jacob attempted to ritualize the spiritual experience so that it could be repeated. He set up an altar, and then, he made a deal: *If* God provided him with food and clothing, and *if* he was returned to his home in peace (the Hebrew is *shalem,* which literally means "whole/intact"), then, and only then, would Adonai be his God. But if not, by implication, he was off the hook. Jacob was seeking physical evidence that the dream was not "just a dream." He wanted proof that it was really God who appeared to him in the night. Like Woody Allen's character in the film *Love and Death,* he wanted "a sign." If only he had a sign, then he would believe, then his faith would be unshakable.

Jacob was young. He was at the beginning of his spiritual journey. And his was an immature faith, a faith that requires tangible reminders of God's reality. The Torah teaches us a very powerful lesson about the nature of the faith journey: Faith does not require proofs or miracles, and proofs do not create faith. This truth was reinforced at Mount Sinai, where an immature people received dramatic proof of God's existence: They saw the parting of the Sea of Reeds, and then they heard the very voice of God. So awesome was this experience that they said to Moses, "Talk to

God, and whatever you say, we will do it and then, later, we will try to comprehend." Yet forty days later, they created a statue out of gold and called it their God! True faith does not require proofs or miracles, and they do not create faith.

Jacob's faith journey, his spiritual awakening, was marked by moments of awareness and certainty, as well as by moments of distance and doubt. So it is for all of us—this is the stuff of true faith. There are moments when the curtains are parted and we know with certainty that we are not alone. We are connected to all that ever was and all that ever will be. We are connected to the One. Perhaps it came at a funeral in the midst of our sadness and grief. A word that someone said or a fleeting memory. Perhaps it was at the birth of your children, witnessing the miracle which is life. Or jogging along familiar paths, chopping veggies at the sink, the way the sun was shining through your office window this afternoon, the dust particles dancing in the air, a certain smell, a song that came on the radio, the chanting of the Hebrew which you have yet to comprehend.

Then there are other moments when we feel so totally alone. When there is no God for us or anyone else. When we need proof, or a sign, or we want to make a deal. Moments of pain, and emptiness, and loss. Doubt is belief's twin. We cannot have the one without the other. And the spiritual journeys of every great tradition are marked with stories of the wilderness or the desert, when all seemed dark or distant, and God's face was hidden from our view.

But this was just the beginning of Jacob's journey. He found the ladder. He had yet to learn how to climb.

As in the lives of many young people, Jacob's relationship to God took a backseat after his initial encounter. Over the course of years, he met and fell in love with Rachel, married and had a family, entered his father-in-law's business, and became quite successful through his shrewdness and acumen. I meet many young couples who tell me that it has been years since they were in a synagogue, but that they will join one when they have children who will need religious school training. When I counsel interfaith couples, they always want to begin with a discussion on how the children will be raised, even before the wedding. Trying to focus the conversation on themselves, I ask them the nature of their religious lives, and the home they are creating. Most often, I get blank stares.

When we're young, at the height of our physical prowess, our attention is focused outward. Our energies are subsumed in the world of matter. We are fully engaged in being creative and procreative, changing and rearranging and fixing the world we encounter. With so many distractions, it's challenging to nourish our inner, spiritual world. When everything's going just right, we may be vaguely aware of God's presence in the background of our daily lives. Jacob knew it was God who gave him children. It was God who allowed him to prosper, the God he met in that first awesome dream. The God of material blessing, the department store God. Just ask, and ye shall receive.

How many of us relate to God in just that way? God exists when we get what we ask for, be it a new car or health for a loved one. God doesn't exist when we turn up empty-handed. Immature spirituality sees God as a dispensary, supplying our every want; those with more are more greatly blessed. The satisfaction of our basic needs is something that we expect, as a prerequisite for life, not something we are thankful for. As the rabbis said, "*Ein kemach, ein Torah*/Without bread, we cannot study Torah."

But as we all know, being well fed and having a roof over our heads is no guarantee there's going to be smooth sailing. And it is through the difficult experiences, life's challenges as well as life's rewards—not separate and apart from them—that our spirituality is formed. Jacob was deceived and mistreated by his father-in-law (and later by his sons). He had to work seven years for a wife he did not want. He was plagued by domestic squabbling and jealousy. He, together with Rachel, faced infertility.

This is real life with real-life problems. And real-life mistakes.

Jacob was not perfect. And his encounter with God was not unlike our own. Momentary, fleeting, now clear, now vague, certain, uncertain. Jacob's awareness of God did not remove him from the bumps, bruises, and scars that mark us and all our lives. It did not remove him from having to live that life. And perhaps most important, it did not remove him from the errors and failures that make us human.

Somehow we have this notion that the spiritual journey has a destination and that once we arrive *there,* we are done. *Parashat Vayetze* (the weekly Torah portion that includes Jacob's leaving his homeland) ends with his setting out to return. This time when Jacob stopped for the night, he saw the angels immediately and named the place *Mahanaim*/God's camp (Genesis 32:3). Jacob had changed: He was God-aware. His prior experience and the years in Haran changed him, though his transformation was not total. As Judaism teaches it, spirituality just doesn't work that way.

Jacob was still flawed, human, untrusting of God and other people. Years later, he sent word to his brother Esau indicating that he had grown quite wealthy in Haran, and that there was something in it for Esau as well. The messengers returned, reporting that Esau was on his way to meet him, together with four hundred men. Jacob, frightened, assumed that Esau was coming to seek his revenge. He lined up troops, and then he talked to God, reminding the Holy One of the promises made to him. He implied in this supplication to God that Adonai's promises of bounty and countless offspring would ring false if his brother destroyed all that Jacob had gained while in Haran.

Are these the actions of one who is spiritually enlightened? Well, yes and no. If we expect that awareness of God leads automatically to unshakable faith, to perfected human interaction, then we will be sorely disappointed in Jacob. Jacob took matters into his own hands; he plotted, schemed, and connived. Even worse, he was still bargaining with God. He had yet to truly believe the promise. And, perhaps Jacob's biggest flaw at that point was his inability to come to terms with his sin against his brother, ascribing the lowest of human motivations to Esau. He was not ready for that encounter.

And so that night, Jacob had to wrestle. The text says his opponent was a man, and perhaps it was. In the morning Jacob believed it was a divine being, an *Elohim,* a God, and he named the place, *Peniel*/The face of God. He saw God, and lived. The prophet Hosea suggested that perhaps it was an angel with whom he wrestled. And modern psychological interpretations have it that Jacob wrestled with himself, his inner demons, his shadow.

What matters was not the adversary, but the process. Once again, Jacob was alone in the wilderness. As opposed to his first encounter with God, this one would not be gentle, but it was awesome. And there was transformation and change.

Jacob was blessed and diminished. He was blessed by having his name changed from *Ya'acov*/Heel grabber to *Yisrael*/The one who strives with God. Throughout the Torah, people and things are named for their characteristics or distinct qualities. I have known a number of people, for example, who have changed their name or taken on a new name in adulthood. Somehow, their birth title no longer fits them, no longer incorporates who they have become. So, too, Jacob's new name allows us to understand him and the nature of his change.

Jacob was also injured in his encounter with the "angel." For the rest of his life, he limps, a reminder to him of his struggle. And a reminder to us that the spiritual journey is fraught with dangers. Life does injure us. We are, each in our own ways, wounded by what life has brought us. Enlightenment also has its price. Not every change is for the better. We are foolish if we think we can travel this path and come away unscathed.

So as Israel, Jacob went to meet his brother, who greeted him with an embrace and kisses. Both brothers wept. Life had been good to Esau, and he had forgiven his brother. In fact, he wanted Jacob to come live with him in Seir. For Esau, the reconciliation was complete. But for Jacob? (It is interesting to note that the Torah does not use his new name of Israel.) He told his brother that he would join him, but never did. Instead, he built his home in Succot, and not Seir. The deceiver still couldn't be honest with his brother. Whether he was guilty or jealous or simply incapable of befriending his brother is unclear. But the sadness is that though Esau (the simple man, the man of the earth, the one who was cheated) was willing to let go of the past, his brother (blessed by God, enlightened) was chained by past behavior. Jacob's character flaw, his inability to deal honestly with people, was not rooted out of him despite his God encounters. Transformation was not total—and apparently, was never completed.

"And so, Jacob, blessed by God, lived happily ever after." There are many people today who search after spirituality secretly expecting such an ending to their story. Calm serenity, inner peace, acceptance, wisdom, knowledge—these are supposed to be the rewards of the life of the spirit. And perhaps they are, for some. But our Torah teaches us that spirituality is not a destination; rather, it is a way, a journey, a path.

Jacob's life in his native land was filled with trouble and pain. The very first story the Torah records after his return to Canaan is the rape of his daughter Dinah and the subsequent slaughter of Hamor and Shechem. Then his beloved Rachel dies during childbirth, and for years, Jacob suffers over the apparent loss of his favorite child, Joseph. Throughout these tales, deception, like a family legacy, weaves a thread. Only toward the very end of his life does Jacob sense some peace. Reunited with Joseph, he lives out his days as a guest of the Egyptian court.

Still, it is during those years that the text records moments of Jacob's continued growth toward the One. He ordered everyone in his household to rid themselves of the gods (i.e., idols) they brought with them from Haran. In the Land of Promise, they would worship only the God who appeared to Jacob in his first dream. Recalling the promise he made, Jacob realized that God had fulfilled all that he asked for. Jacob rededicated the altar in *Beth El,* and God appeared to him to reaffirm the promise and to change his name, once again, to Israel.

If we read this as a single narrative (modern biblical scholars believe that two different versions of the text account for the two name changes), we see that heights once reached in the spiritual journey will have to be assailed again and again. There are lessons we all need to learn over and over again. It is true of our psyches and our souls. Sure, Jacob's name was changed to Israel in a dramatic encounter along a riverbank. How many of us have had life transformations in a moment of time? But becoming Israel, truly becoming that new person, can take a lifetime.

Our name, our essence, the things we identify ourselves with, will change over the course of our lives. They don't change once and for all time unless we cease to grow and evolve and experience. Like a Zen garden, the path will wind its way around and about, up and down, in and out—with no real end. We're not seeking "perfection" because we don't need to be perfect to encounter the Divine. And truly finding God will not render us perfect.

We are all Jacob/Israel. That is literally one of our Jewish names—*B'nai Yisrael*/Children of Israel—and that is our spiritual reality. Like Jacob, we are all on a journey, destination uncertain. That is why you have this book in your hand. And that is why I have written it. By sharing my journey with you, we become partners, easing the loneliness and the pain we experience along the way. I have been wounded and so have you. Most of the time we try to hide those scars, but even the toughest of us has to limp sometimes. Yet, there are moments when the way seems clear and we know where we are headed. There are connections we make, with others and with God, that light the path and steady our steps. Antiphonal moments, mundane moments, moments of crisis, and moments of joy. Moments that we work toward, and moments that surprise us and catch us unawares. Moments that bring a smile to our lips and moments that strike terror in our hearts. We are Jacob, an ordinary and imperfect human being touched by moments of greatness. That is our certain inheritance and our birthright.

   I was counseling a congregant in spiritual growth and we came to a very painful realization. She was talking about how she "used to" behave in relationships and new experiences, always testing the waters, always keeping one foot out the door, just in case. "A control game?" I suggested. Suddenly she recognized that she was still doing it. "But I was done with that!" And then we laughed . . . laughed until we cried. Jewish spirituality is not someplace out there. It does not free us or exempt us from having to make the journey. Nor does it spare us from the inevitable pain which makes up so much of life itself. It does not make us perfect. But it is an awareness . . . that we are not all there is . . . that there is this "something" greater than us, than all our crea-tions . . . a Transcendent reality who has been called by many names . . . the One who has carried us and will hold us close . . . the Eternal Presence who is everywhere at all times. This awareness can be fleeting. It can be accepted or denied. Or we can work to make it the defining reality of our lives.

The Workout

Most people go for annual physical exams as well as to the gym to stay in peak physical condition. Likewise, when it comes to maintaining our psyches, we have self-help books, support groups, and trained professionals there to guide us. To keep our minds sharp, we have courses, books, magazines, and all manner of educational programming. But when it comes to our spirits, our souls, somehow we expect them to be healthy all by themselves.

Every religious tradition provides for daily contact with God. In Judaism, this has meant three worship services (morning, afternoon, and evening). An alternative tradition notes that we ought to find opportunities to say a hundred blessings every day, which includes those said during formal worship. If God is the energy source of the universe, then it is as if we need to plug in our batteries to be recharged each day. Or, understanding God as intimate friend or lover, we want to check in with one another on a regular basis. For some, this will mean attending a regular minyan—the quorum of ten adult Jews required for communal worship—each day. For others, an annual pilgrimage to the synagogue will meet their need. But many of us would like an opportunity for a daily, meaningful connection that fits into the reality of our very busy lives. It is to that end that the Ten-Minute Workout was created.

This workout is designed to work on your connection to self and to the Transcendent Power of the Universe we call God. It consists of some basic prayers and blessings that were originally meant to be said at home, and a meditation of the day whose theme is linked to the Jewish calendar cycle. There are also some optional prayers and rituals you may do to enhance your workout. You can find them in this section or in the Appendix. Each workout is designed to end with the prayer known as the *Sh'ma*. I have included six meditations per theme because it is my belief that at least one day a week, preferably Shabbat, we ought to feed off the energy of being in community. Though spirit work is often lonely, ultimately we cannot do this work all by ourselves. To connect with other travelers enhances our journey.

I have called this a workout because it is designed to be done at home or at the office, anytime of day, by yourself or with others, by itself or in conjunction with other focused activities (like exercising). Besides, whether or not we visit the gym, we all know what a workout is. As with a physical regimen, benefit is accrued with regular praxis, even if the results do not appear immediately. As we know from daily physical exercise, one does not have to work out for hours in order to achieve the desired outcome. Regular repetition is the most important feature. God is everywhere, always accessible to us. Ten minutes is enough time to make that awareness and connection.

The meditation themes are organized according to the time line of the Torah. Though we are used to beginning the year with Rosh Hashanah or January 1, the Torah understands that life begins in spring. Since cyclical time is meant to be repeated each year as a microcosm of our own life cycle, I chose to begin with spring as well. I suggest that no matter when you begin this book, you do stay "in season." It will make more sense that way.

DAILY PRAYERS

The following prayers are to be read or recited every day as part of the workout. You can think about the "prompts" preceding the prayers, read or chant the prayer aloud in English or in Hebrew (transliterations are provided). Feel free to incorporate traditional melodies or to make up your own. Instruments, movement, or simple drumming may also enhance your workout.

MODEH AHNI

Think of something for which you are grateful today. Say thanks.
I am grateful to You, Giver and Sustainer of life, for having granted me another day of life. Your love and faith in me is truly overwhelming.
MO'DEH AH'NI L'FA'NE'CHA MELECH CHAI V'KA'YAM SHEH'CHEH'ZAR'TAH BEE NISH'MAH'TEE B'CHEM'LAH RA'BAH EH'MOO'NAH'TEH'CHA.

THE DAILY CHECK-IN WITH SELF

The human being is a complex organism made up of many different forces. Though, as Jews, we recognize the interconnected nature of all these, when we check in with ourselves, we do so one part at a time.

OUR BODIES/HEALTH

Think about your body's health. Be mindful of all the ways it is functioning, even when some parts are not.
Blessed are You, Adonai our God, Ruler of the Universe, who has made our bodies with wisdom, complete with veins, arteries, glands, valves, and organs. We know that if one were to be open when it should be closed, or closed when it should open, it would be impossible to exist or to stand before You. Blessed are you, Adonai, Healer of all flesh, who sustains us in wondrous ways.
BARUCH ATAH ADONAI ELOHEINU MELECH HA'OH'- LAM AH'SHER YA'TZAR ET-HA'AH'DAM B'CHOCH'MAH,

OO'VAH'RAH VO N'KAH'VEEM N'KAH'VEEM, CHA'LOO'-
LEEM CHA'LOO'LEEM. GAH'LOUIE V'YAH'DOO'AH
LEEF'NAI CHEE'SAY CH'VO'DEH'CHA SH'EEM YEE'PAH'-
TAY'ACH EH'CHAD MAY'HEM OH YEE'SAH'TAIM EH'CHAD
MAY'HEM, EE EF'SHAR L'TEET'KAH'YAIM V'LA'AH'MODE
L'FA'NEH'CHA. BA'RUCH AH'TAH ADONAI ROE'FAY
CHOL BA'SAR OO'MAF'LEE LA'AH'SOTE.

OUR MINDS / TORAH

Think about your mind. Be aware of its ability to study and incorporate new concepts and ideas.

Blessed are You, Adonai our God, Ruler of the Universe, who makes us holy through *mitzvot*/commandments, and calls us to immerse ourselves in the words of Torah. May the words of Torah be sweet in our mouths and in the mouths of all the household of Israel, so that we and our children may come to love You and study Your holy words. Blessed are You, Adonai, our Teacher of Torah.

BARUCH AH'TAH ADONAI ELOHEINU MELECH HA'OH'-
LAM AH'SHER KID'SHA'NU B'MITZ'VO'TAV V'TZI'VAH'NU
LA'AH'SOKE B'DEEV'RAY TORAH. V'HA'AH'REV-NAH,
ADONAI ELOHEINU, ET-DEEV'RAY TOE'RAH'TEH'CHA
B'FEE'NOO, OO'V'FEE AHM'CHA BAIT YIS'RAH'ALE,
V'NEE'H'YEH AH'NACH'NOO V'TZEH'EH'TZAH'AI'NOO,
V'TZEH'EH'TZAH'AI AHM'CHA BAIT YIS'RAH'ALE,
KOO'LA'NOO YODE'AI SH'MEH'CHA V'LOME'DAY TOE'-
RAH'TEH'CHA LEESH'MA. BARUCH AH'TAH ADONAI,
HA'M'LA'MADE TORAH L'AH'MOE YIS'RAH'ALE.

(NOTE: *Mitzvah* (or the plural *mitzvot*) is used colloquially to mean "good deed," but in this book we will use the literal definition of commandment.)

OUR HEARTS/BEHAVIOR

Think about what you do each day, each week. How many actions do you take on behalf of another person? How many things do you do to make the world a better place in which to live? (Read or chant the traditional list that follows. Add to it from your own experience.)

AI'LOO D'VARIM SH'EIN LA'HEM SHE'OOR, SH'AH'-DAM OH'CHAIL PAY'RO'TAY'HEM BA'OH'LAM HA'ZEH V'HA'KEH'REN KA'YEH'MET LO LA'OH'LAM HA'BA, V'AY'-LOO HAYN:

These are some of the unlimited ways that our hearts may lead us to serve:

Honor father and mother
KEE'BOOD AV V'AIM
Perform acts of love and kindness
OOG'ME'LOOT CHA'SA'DEEM
Study with others each day
*V'HASH'KA'MAHT BAIT HA'MEED'RASH SHA'CHA'REET
   V'AHR'VEET*
Welcome strangers and guests
V'HACH'NAH'SAHT OR'CHEEM
Visit the sick
OO'VEE'KOOR CHO'LEEM
Rejoice with bride and groom
V'HACH'NAH'SAHT KAH'LAH
Console the bereaved
OOL'VAH'YAT HA'MATE
Pray with sincerity
V'EE'YOUN T'FEE'LAH
Make peace between people
*VAH'HAVAH'AHT SHA'LOME BAIN AH'DAM
   LA'CHA'VAY'ROE*

But know that our study of Torah should lead us to act
V'TAL'MOOD TOE'RAH K'NEH'GED KOO'LAHM.

OUR SPIRITUAL ENERGY/SOUL

*Think about what makes you uniquely you. Then feel the life
force flowing in and out of you as you breathe deeply, inhaling
through your nose and exhaling through your mouth.*

My God, the soul that you have implanted within me is pure.
You created and formed it, breathed it into me, and sustain it each
and every day. So long as I have life, I will be grateful to You,
Adonai my God and God of my mother and father, Creator of all
life, Sustainer of every human spirit. Blessed are You, Adonai, in
whose hands are the souls of all life, and the spirits of all flesh.
*EH'LO'HIGH, N'SHA, MAH SH'NAH'TA'TA BEE T'HOE'-
RAH HEE! AH'TAH B'RAH'TAH, AH'TAH Y'TZAR'TAH,
AH'TAH N'FACH'TAH BEE, V'AH'TAH M'SHAM'RAH
B'KEER'BEE. KOL-Z'MAN SH'HAN'SHA'MAH B'KEER'BEE,
MO'DEH AH'NEE L'FA'NEH'CHA, ADONAI EH'LO'HAY
AH'VO'TAI V'EE'MO'TAI, REE'BONE KOL-HA'MA'AH'SEEM,
AH'DOHN KOL-HA'N'SHA'MOTE.
BARUCH AH'TAH ADONAI AH'SHER B'YA'DOE NEH'FESH
KOL CHAI, V'ROO'ACH KOL B'SAR EESH.*

MEDITATION OF THE DAY

Sh'ma
You should end every workout with the *Sh'ma.*
As you say the *Sh'ma,* think about how you and all of creation
are one.

Hear O Israel, Adonai, and only Adonai, Is our God
SH'MA YISRAEL, ADONAI ELOHEINU, ADONAI ECHAD

Blessed be God's glorious name forever and ever
BARUCH SHEM K'VOD MALCHUTO L'OLAM VA'ED

All the meditations are arranged by themes, organized according to the seasons and the Jewish calendar, six meditations per theme. In order to select the Meditation of the Day, you may want to use a Jewish calendar or simply pick the theme that feels most compelling. Read the selection once or twice, including the meditation question or exercise. Meditation simply means focused energy. With eyes closed, and slow, deep breathing (in through your nose and out through your mouth) consider the meditation question. If your mind drifts, bring it back to the question. Do this for as long as you need to do so. After opening your eyes, you may want to write down some of your thoughts or insights. Then complete the workout by saying or chanting the *Sh'ma*.

OPTIONAL BLESSINGS AND RITUALS

The following prayers and rituals may be incorporated into your workout if you have some extra time or if you feel the need. You can include them every day, intermittently, or not at all.

TALLIT AND TEFILLIN

The tallit and tefillin are ways of bringing ourselves closer to God—physical reminders, tangible symbols of our relationship with the Holy One. Whether or not you use these "prayer phenalia," think about the ways you can feel the presence of God in your life, and how you can bring God closer.

(NOTE: A tallit/prayer shawl, wrapped around our shoulders or draped over our heads, can help us feel the enveloping presence of God. A blanket or shawl can be used instead. Tefillin/prayer phylacteries are leather straps used to "bind us" to God. They are available in most Judaica shops. Instructions for their use can be found in *The First Jewish Catalog* by Strassfeld, Strassfeld, and Siegel.)

Either before or after saying thanks (*MODEH AHNI*), wrap yourself in your tallit and say:

"Praise Adonai, O my soul!
Adonai, my God, You are very great!
Arrayed in glory and majesty
You wrap Yourself in light as if it were a garment
You stretch out the heavens like a curtain."

Blessed are You, Adonai our God, Ruler of the Universe, who makes us holy with *mitzvot*/commandments, and calls us to wrap ourselves in the *tzitzit*/fringes of the tallit.

BARUCH AH'TAH ADONAI ELOHEINU MELECH HA'-OLAM, AH'SHER KID'SHA'NU B'MITZ'VO'TAV V'TZI'-VAH'NU L'HEET'AH'TAIF BA'TZI'TZIT.

Wrap yourself in your tefillin and say:

Blessed are You, Adonai our God, Ruler of the Universe, who makes us holy with *mitzvot*/commandments, and calls us to wrap our arms and head with tefillin.

BARUCH AH'TAH ADONAI ELOHEINU MELECH HA'-OLAM AH'SHER KID'SHA'NU B'MITZ'VO'TAV V'TZI'-VAH'NU L'HA'NEE'ACH T'FEE'LEEN.

PSALM OF THE DAY

The Psalms express many moods and can comfort, inspire, or provoke you, depending on the need. If you feel like you want to expand on your workout on any given day, you can reflect on the following psalms:

When God seems far away . . . Psalm 139
When you are discouraged . . . Psalm 40
When you are lonely or fearful . . . Psalm 23
When you forget your blessings . . . Psalm 103
When the world seems bigger than God . . . Psalm 90

When your prayers grow narrow or self-centered. . . .
   Psalm 67
When people fail you. . . . Psalm 27
When you have sinned. . . . Psalm 51
When you are in danger. . . . Psalm 91
When you are depressed. . . . Psalm 34
When all seems lost. . . . Psalm 6 or 13
When you are in trouble. . . . Psalm 86

Healing Prayer—Mi Sheberach

If you know of someone who is in physical, emotional, and/or spiritual pain, yourself included, you may want to add on his/her behalf:

> Heal us and we shall be healed
> Save us and we shall be saved
>
> *Vee'hee ra'tzon meel'fa'ne'cha Adonai*
> *Eloheinu vay 'lohei avoteinu v'imoteinu*
> *Sh'teesh 'lach r'fu'ah shlei'mah min ha'sha'ma'yim*
> *r'fu'at ha'nefesh v'r'fu'at ha'goof*
>
> Faithful God, Compassionate One
> We are broken and in pain
> Our loved ones call out to us
> So we call out to You
> Heal us
> Make us whole
> Let us know peace.

(If you are praying for someone who is ill, you may add):

May it be Your will, Adonai our God and God of our Mothers and Fathers, to send perfect healing to _____ , along with all others who are stricken. For You are the faithful and merciful God of healing. Blessed are You, Eternal One, Healer of Your people Israel.

Nightly Meditation—Hashkivenu

The night is a time of darkness and danger and fear. Think of all the things that frighten you (for yourself, your family, the world) and ask for God's protection and love.

Hashkivenu Adonai Eloheinu
May we lie down this night
in safety and in peace
May we wake each day
to life and to love

Ufros aleinu sukkat shlomecha
May we spend our days
in Your sheltering presence
protected from all evil
sadness, danger, and harm.

U'shmor tzei'tei'nu u'vo'einu
May we journey through life
in the shadow of your wings
O God of compassion
our Shield and Salvation
now and forever.
Amen.

SPRING

PURIM

~

When Purim arrives we realize winter is (almost) over and we are still alive! This is cause to celebrate. And celebrate we do, by finding our inner child and letting it go wild. That is why we wear a mask. It gives us the freedom to be our alter ego or anything else we want to be. Exactly one month later, it is that child who will open the door for Elijah at the Passover seder. The story of Purim does not mention God by name. Why should we?

meditations
RISK TAKING

And Mordechai answered Esther, "Do not think in your heart that you shall escape in the king's house any more than all the other Jews. For if you remain silent in this time, relief and deliverance will arise from another source but you and your father's house will perish; and who knows whether or not it was for such a moment as this that you came to be queen?"
— ESTHER 4:13—14

There are moments in each of our lives when we must decide a course of action, or make a choice between equally compelling possibilities. It may concern a career option, a commitment to a relationship, a place to live, or a school to attend. But we know that whatever we decide, and even if we fail to decide, life will never quite be the same again. And when our story is told, it will be this moment, and other moments like it, that will give shape and substance to who we are and what we have become. I am not sure that one can ever prepare for such a moment, for no one really knows when it will occur. We just walk to the edge, and jump off. Perhaps it may help to trust that God will be there to catch us, if, in fact, we do stumble and fall.

Think about a time when you had to make a life-changing decision. Do you remember how it felt? Do you remember how you made it? What gave you the strength to let go?

No great task will ever be undertaken if all possible objections must first be overcome.

— NATHAN CUMMINGS

No one wants to be reckless. We do not want to risk all that we have accomplished, all that we have gained, all that we have worked so hard to acquire. Yet we would not have gotten there unless we had taken some chances, gambled with our time and resources, lived with some doubt and uncertainty. And the bigger the challenge, the greater the risk involved.

We must do due diligence before any undertaking. This is healthy. This reflects maturity and wisdom. But we must be careful not to allow that caution to turn into paralysis of action, lest we never do that which we can, that which we ought to do.

What challenges await your action? Have you overcome most objections? Are you hesitating because you have not overcome them all?

The significant problems we face cannot be solved at the same level of thinking we were at when we created them.

— ALBERT EINSTEIN

Where there is life, there are problems. That is just the way it is. No life is problem-free. And a big part of the task of being human is grappling with, and (one hopes) overcoming, that which besets us. Unfortunately, most of us think that problems come from forces outside ourselves. The truth is, we are the source of both the problem *and* the solution. And if we want to solve any of our significant problems, the really sticky ones, we will have to recognize our role in creating them, and then step outside of ourselves to work on their resolution.

Such a step is scary, and so most of us become paralyzed, blaming others, blaming forces beyond our control, when really it is up to us. But we have to change. We have to look with a new heart, a new mind-set, a willingness to face our problems as challenges to our growth and creativity.

Think of the significant problems you now face. (Go ahead, we all have problems.) For each one, recognize the role you played in creating it. Then, pretending you are someone else, determine how that person would solve it. (If you want, you could make a three-column chart—Problem, Role I Played, Solution. Sometimes, it helps to see things written out that way.)

Proactive means more than merely taking initiative. It means that as human beings, we are responsible for our own lives. It means our behavior is a function of our decisions, not our conditions; our values, not our feelings.

— STEPHEN COVEY

"Proactive" is one of today's buzzwords. In all endeavors, we seek people who can be proactive, which we associate with "taking charge" of things. But it is really more than that. And it begins with responsibility. Yes, there are forces out there beyond our control. Yes, there are randomness and accidents and evil, and all of those can effect us, even hurt us from time to time. Nevertheless, the life we live is, by and large, our creation. And we can create that life out of our essential self and our core values, or we can allow that life to be shaped by others, by the conditions under which we live, by the feelings that are not under our control. It really and truly is up to us. It all depends on how we want to live our lives.

Are there still parts of your life for which you have yet to take responsibility? Things you are blaming on others, on "forces beyond your control," on God? For each of those aspects of your life, list the decisions you need to make in order to effect change. Also, list the values you hold sacred that you could bring to each of these aspects. (This could also be a chart. Five columns: Areas in Which I Am Not Taking Responsibility, Conditions I Blame, Decisions I Need to Make, Feelings That Get in the Way, Values I Could Bring.)

> *As we are liberated from our own fear,*
> *our presence automatically liberates others.*
> — NELSON MANDELA

Fear and indecision are an intrinsic part of the human condition. How often are we confronted by choices and challenges? How often, influenced by our doubts and fears, do we travel the well-worn path? How often do we let our fears dictate our course? This is not to say that the well-worn path is always wrong. Sometimes, that is exactly where we belong. But only when we make the decision out of our values, knowing what our options are, knowing who we are.

To take the path that few have traveled is always a risk. To take the path that we have not yet traveled is also a risk. But it is in such risks that the texture and contour of life is created. Know that no one is ever alone when taking these risks. God goes with us in every step, on every path. And others will follow.

What risks are confronting you now? Which path awaits your first step?

Thus all life represents a risk, and the more lovingly we live our lives, the more risks we take.

— M. SCOTT PECK

To live is a risk. To love is a risk. In fact, anytime we open ourselves to pain or hurt, disappointment or failure, anytime the outcome is uncertain, anytime we extend ourselves beyond what we thought possible, we are taking a risk. We can try to make it not so. We can try to live our lives in such a way that everything will be predictable and known, but beyond the impossibility of such a life, would it really be one worth living? Is that what we really want?

We need to risk. And we need to love. To live our lives as lovingly as we possibly can. And while we will not be reckless, we know that there will be times when we are frightened or overwhelmed. But this will not deter us, or stop us from living or loving. So, what risks are confronting you now? Where are you holding back? When will you take those first steps? Put it on your calendar.

❧   ❧   ❧

m e d i t a t i o n s

MAZAL/LUCK

In the first month . . . they cast pur—that is, "the lot"—before Haman, from day to day, and from month to month.

— ESTHER 3:7

Sometimes it comes down to just this. The casting of sticks, a roll of the dice, a decision not made, a road not taken. There is an element of chance in life, in all our lives, and everything, all that we worked for, all that we have gained, hangs in the balance. That is what we celebrate on Purim. Our "lot" was to be destroyed. Yet somehow, we managed to escape. Unlike the exodus from Egypt, in which we were freed by God's "outstretched arm and mighty hand," in Purim we are left to our own devices, and for this, we need a bit of luck.

Purim, "lots," a casting of divining sticks falling where they may. How many of our lives turned on such a moment? How many of us needed a bit of luck to escape some hazard along the way? How many of us are here, reading these words, because of some good fortune at a moment when we least expected it? How many have suffered because, through no fault of our own, we were simply in the wrong place at the wrong time?

Think about a time when luck seemed to pull you through. Think about how it might have been otherwise. Think about it and be grateful.

Rava said, "Length of life, children, and sustenance depend not on merit but on mazal."

— TALMUD, MOED KATAN 28A

Many of our self-help books would have us think that everything is a matter of our effort and hard work—that if we want something badly enough, then there is nothing to stop us from going out there and getting it. Nothing, that is, except ourselves. We can beat that cancer, make that fortune, have that baby, choose our body type . . . you name it, we can have it, if only we will it. The second-century sage Rava told us differently. He said there are certain things in life that are beyond our control. Certain things that have nothing to do with our will or our effort. Certain things that are dependent on luck, pure and simple. He was thinking of two colleagues, Rabbah and Hisda, both of whom were righteous men, yet one had a long life full of blessing, while the other died young after a life of trouble and sorrow. We all know such people. Perhaps you are one of them. Despite your best efforts, there are areas of your life in which you continually fail. Luck is part of the fabric of the universe.

Are there areas in your life in which you feel lucky? Think about them and be grateful. Are there areas in which you feel unlucky? Stop blaming yourself.

Mazel exists only to wreak havoc on the natural order, into which it weaves its way like smoke, coupling and uncoupling events for no reason that goes beyond itself, the "causa sui" of chance and disorder.
— FROM *MAZEL*, BY REBECCA GOLDSTEIN

There is a natural order which is regular and dependable. The sun comes up in the morning and goes down at night. Fish swim and birds fly and most of us go about the business of living most of the time. We can rely upon this order, this regularity; we can and do build our lives around it. Yet even if we are only casual observers of life, we have to admit that there is a certain amount of randomness built into the world as well. Accidents happen. Young people can get sick and die. Loved ones get caught in the wrong place at the wrong time. That is just the way it is. It is not all fixed and orderly. Things just happen, sometimes.

Imagine your life as a geometric pattern, stretching forth as far as your eye can see . . . Examine those parts of the pattern that are irregular, broken, or incomplete. That is *mazal*, sometimes for the good, and sometimes for the bad.

(NOTE: "Mazel" is the Yiddish spelling and pronunciation; "mazal" is the Hebrew.)

He who says, "Be lucky, my luck, and tire not by day or night," is guilty of Amorite practices.
— TALMUD, SHABBAT 67B

I grew up hearing the words *k'ayin ha'ra* (pronounced *kina hara;* literal meaning, "no evil eye") said after anyone mentioned anything positive about anyone else. "He's getting so tall, *k'ayin ha'ra* . . . She's doing well in school, *k'ayin ha'ra* . . . You have such good kids, *k'ayin ha'ra*." It was meant as a protection, so that nothing should happen to change the course of that positive attribute or happening.

While luck may be a factor of the universe, praying for it, or trying to influence it through our actions, is supposed to be un-Jewish ("pooh pooh pooh," as Jewish people often say). Yet how many of us dip apples in honey at Rosh Hashanah so that we can have a sweet year, or break a glass at a wedding (meant to drive away the evil spirits that come to spoil the happiness), or don't tell someone we are ill until the second day? Trying to change our luck or influence it for the good may be mired in superstition, but it is human nature to do so anyway.

What do you do to keep away the "evil spirits"? How do you try to influence your luck for the good?

Throw a lucky man into the sea, and he will come up with a pearl in his hand.

— LADINO FOLK SAYING

Don't you know people like that? No matter what they do, it always seems to come out right. And there are others whom we say have "no *mazal*." They seem to spend their entire lives with a black cloud hanging over them. Of course, it is not fair, but it seems to describe reality, nonetheless.

There are some people who are just plain lucky, and it has nothing to do with their character, personality, or ethical standards.

Do you consider yourself a lucky or unlucky person? How do you know?

The harder I work, the luckier I get.
— SAMUEL GOLDWYN

Oh, that Jewish skepticism! Is it really luck, or is that just an excuse for our personal failures? Does luck really play a factor in anything I do? The word *mazal* in Hebrew literally means "star." Does astrology play a role in determining the outcome of my life? Should I be checking the newspaper each morning before I venture out into the world? Or would I be better off utilizing that same energy simply to work harder? Forget about all this talk about luck!

Or perhaps we can read this another way. As I work harder, I do seem to get more breaks. More things seem to go my way. Perhaps the one does influence the other. Perhaps they go hand in hand.

Has that been your experience as well? That the harder you work, the luckier you get? Or are the two totally unrelated in your life? Be honest with yourself.

❧   ❧   ❧

m e d i t a t i o n s
SELF-ESTEEM/SELF-RELIANCE

The spies reported to Moses that the inhabitants of Canaan were such giants that "We appeared to them as grasshoppers, and that is how we were in our own eyes." This teaches us that the esteem you receive from others depends on how much you value yourself.

— RABBI YITZHAK MEIR OF GUR

We have heard this basic truth in so many different ways. No one can truly love us unless we first love ourselves . . . no one will respect us unless we have self-respect . . . and now we read that the esteem we receive from others also depends on having self-esteem. It always begins with the self.

Unlike some religious systems, Judaism does not ask that we crush or wipe out our egos. We do not need to eliminate our sense of self or eliminate our individuality. Rather, Judaism asks that we keep it under control, directing our ego strength toward honest evaluation and healthy, positive endeavors. Self-esteem, knowing what we are and what we are not, and valuing that, is the beginning of healthy ego.

There were twelve spies. All were princes and leaders of their tribes. All had been slaves in Egypt. Ten had not yet overcome their slave experience; their self-esteem was wounded and they could not imagine themselves taking over the Land of Promise, despite God's and Moses' assurances. But two spies tried to encourage the people to fight for what was theirs by birthright. So, while we are shaped by our childhood experiences, we do not need to be controlled by them. We can see ourselves as "grasshoppers," or we can see ourselves as we truly are.

How are you feeling about yourself, right now? If we asked ten people to describe you (some strangers, some friends), what would they say?

> *What lies behind us and what lies before us are tiny matters compared to what lies within us.*
>
> — OLIVER WENDELL HOLMES

To some extent, we are all shaped by our experiences and the conditions of our environment. To some extent, the past and the future put contours on our lives. But this is not the essence of who we are and what we are truly about. That can only come from within. Spring is a time of new beginnings. The winter hibernation is over. Each day, there is more light. It is time to take stock of ourselves and see what lies within. This will prepare us for the work that lies ahead.

What is inside you now? Take a good look. Close your eyes and you will see.

Before he died, Rabbi Zusya said, "In the world to come they will not ask me, 'Why were you not Moses?' They will ask me, 'Why were you not Zusya?'"
— (ATTRIBUTED TO) ZUSYA OF HANIPOLI

We go around thinking we have to be like somebody else, comparing ourselves with others, living up to another's standard or expectation. We drive ourselves crazy by thinking that no matter what we do or accomplish, somehow it is just not good enough, when all along all that God wants of us is that we be ourselves. You be you and I will be me. That's all. That is enough.

How simple it is, and yet how difficult we make it.

So who are you trying to be? What image of yourself are you trying to live up to? Are you ready to stop and just be yourself? Before you begin your meditation today, announce who you are. Dear God, I am _____, son/daughter of _____ . That is all you have to be. Today and every day.

I am only one, but I am one. I cannot do everything, but I can do something. What I can do, I ought to do. And what I ought to do, by God's grace, I will do.
— AUTHOR UNKNOWN

I am one and I can do something. What a great place for our self-esteem to begin. And not a bad place for it to end up, either. We cannot do it all and we do not have to kill ourselves trying. There is no one who can do it all. Forget that notion. But we can do something. And with God's help, we will. In fact, I am sure we do.

Reflect on all that you do. Think about just one day in your life.

Think of the people with whom you interact—partners, children, family, friends, coworkers, clients. Think of all that you add to their lives. Think of all that you can and will do today.

I know of no more encouraging fact than the unquestionable ability of man to elevate his life by conscious endeavor.
                                        — HENRY DAVID THOREAU

Our lives are not programmed. There is no fate determining our every move. In fact, we are freely choosing, conscious individuals, writing the script to our own lives each and every day. And our primary mode of doing so is through our behavior, our actions. We may not have any control over our feelings; we do not invite ourselves to love or hate, to feel joy or sadness. Our random thoughts come and go as they please, often surprising us as much as anyone else. But what we do in normal healthy functioning, that is our choice. Always. And our lives can be changed, improved, elevated through those choices.

What is it that you have been wanting to do that has the potential to enhance your self-esteem? Make a plan. Start today.

Yet we are Your people, children of Your covenant, and it is we that You have called to Your service.
                                        — DAILY MORNING PRAYER

One of the ways the Jewish people survived centuries of oppression was to remind themselves each day (perhaps they were reminding God as well) that they were God's people, children of the covenant, and that no matter what their outward circumstances were, they had a higher purpose toward which to strive. That is powerful medicine for someone living in a ghetto, exiled from land to land, barely making enough to stay alive. It is powerful medicine for us as well, who, despite our success and material wealth, often feel adrift and without purpose. We are God's people. Each and every one of us. We are Adonai's children. And we have work to do.

What is it that God is calling you to do today? If you are not sure, ask. "Adonai, what is it that You are calling me, Your son/daughter, to do today?"

~ ~ ~

meditations

CLEANING OUT THE HAMETZ/LETTING GO

Blessed are You, Adonai our God, Ruler of the Universe, who makes our lives holy with Your commandments, and has commanded us to remove all the hametz in our possession.
— PRAYER BEFORE THE SEARCH FOR *HAMETZ*

The countdown has begun. We have tethered our lambs and marked our doors with blood, indicating our desire to be free. Soon, Moses has promised, the redemption will begin. There is just one more thing: We must rid ourselves of every trace of *hametz/* leaven. Anyone caught with *hametz* during these next seven days will be *karait,* cut off from his/her people for seven generations, a punishment far worse than death. Begin your search.

So, why all this fuss about some bread and cookies? Why do we begin this process a full month before Passover? Why are we not even supposed to have it around during the seven days of the festival? Unlike *traif* (nonkosher foods like pork and shellfish), *hametz* is permissible food, forbidden only during Passover. And the truth is, we don't really want to get rid of it. But *hametz* is a symbol of our slavery, that which ties us down to Egypt. It is our addictions and our weaknesses, our fears and our doubts. It is what will make us want to return to Egypt the moment things get rough. It is the goodies with which we love to indulge ourselves.

It is one thing to distance oneself from that which is clearly unhealthy (and even that can be tricky at times); it is quite another to take control of that which is normatively a part of our lives but cannot be for a period of time. That is the challenge of *hametz.* Taking control of our lives.

Where is the *hametz* in your life? Make a list. Then get rid of everything on it.

It is one's duty to conduct the examination (for hametz) at night.
— MOSES MAIMONIDES (RAMBAM)

It is with a certain amount of ambivalence that we carry out this process of searching for *hametz.* After all, we rationalize, these foodstuffs are not really forbidden; we eat them all year round. What harm would there be if we kept a little around during Passover, just in case we felt the desire? That is why we do the search at night. We cannot use the darkness as our excuse. We cannot say, "I just didn't see it." In fact, it is the search itself that brings light to all the darkened corners of our lives. *Hametz* is insidious in hiding itself from our view. We need to be thorough in our search.

One of the great ironics of our existence is that letting go means taking control. We cannot let go of anything unless it belongs to us. Getting rid of the *hametz* is an act of will. It indicates our desire to take control of our lives and to ready ourselves for the new year of life that begins in spring. Where is the *hametz* hiding in your life? What light can you bring to uncover/discover it?

Hametz indicates a process occurring without the formative guidance of its maker.
— RABBI TZVI ELIMELECH OF LYZHENSK

Anything can become its opposite. Because the truth is, opposites are often two sides of the same coin, not very far apart at all. The real difference between matzah and *hametz* (besides texture and taste) is that *hametz* rises on its own, while matzah is proof that no spontaneous activity has taken place. To prevent *hametz* from taking place requires a great deal of watchfulness, of focused energy, of concentrated effort. For you see, according to our sages, even "matzah dough can become *hametz* if the process of rising is permitted to begin" (Shulhen Aruch, Orach Chaim 45a). That's because they begin in exactly the same way—flour and water. They can be made from the same exact dough.

And so it is with almost all our endeavors in life. A slip here or there, a moment of carelessness, an assumption that does not materialize, and we are stuck with something we did not intend. Passover calls on us to get down to the basics, the simplest substances of life. There are so many distractions. How did it get that way? What are you living with that you did not intend? What has become *hametz* for you when you weren't even looking? Passover is approaching. Time to get rid of it.

But as for the deeper meaning, that which is leavened and fermented rises, while that which is unleavened is low. Each of these is a symbol of types of soul, one being haughty and swollen with arrogance, the other being unchangeable and prudent, choosing the middle way rather than extremes because of desire and zeal for equality.

— Philo of Alexandria

And you thought it was just a piece of bread! I am reminded of the biblical battle that takes place between Moses and Pharaoh. (Even if you did not read the book, you probably saw the movie—Charlton Heston and Yul Brynner.) In spite of all the signs, in spite of all the destruction all around him, in spite of the fact that every one of his advisers is telling him to get rid of these people, Pharaoh is unable to let them go. He cannot admit defeat. And even after he sends them on their way he regrets his action, and chases them, to his own death. This is the stuff of real tragedy. Pharaoh's ego, his pride, his inability to understand that he really is not God after all all lead to his downfall and demise.

Passover calls on us to shed all the parts of ourselves that are puffed up with false pride. We need to be on guard against all the self-righteousness that distorts who we are and what we are all about. Passover calls on us to become more "matzohlike," to get down to our basic self. So where are you "puffed up"? Where have you distorted your importance? Your power? Your role in life? That is *hametz*. Get rid of it.

> *Leaven and unleaven symbolize the evil and good inclinations in people.*
> — THE ZOHAR, FROM THE BOOK OF SPLENDOR, MOSES DE LEON

We might as well admit it: Each of us has the capacity for great good, and great evil as well. They are both forces in every human being. We are born with them. And they are with us until the day we die. Our job is not to eliminate the inclination to do evil, for that is an impossibility. Rather, our task is to try to control it. That, and nothing more. Most of us do a very good job of it, most of the time. And most of the evils we do commit are fairly innocuous. Nevertheless, all we have to do is read the newspaper to realize that even good people do terrible things each and every day.

By getting rid of the *hametz* before Passover, we make a statement (to God and to ourselves) about our battle with the evil inclination within ourselves. Though we know there is no ultimate getting rid of all the *hametz* in our world, at least for these seven days we can (temporarily) triumph. And as Passover serves as a precursor to the messianic redemption we seek, a time when good will vanquish evil (that is why the door is opened for Elijah the prophet), we get a foretaste of that time by getting rid of our *hametz*.

With each item of *hametz* that you burn, put away, throw out, sell, imagine your inclination to do evil draining out of you.

All the hametz that may be in my possession, whether I have removed it or not, is hereby nullified and ownerless as the dust of the earth.

— PRAYER UPON BURNING OF *HAMETZ*

Even after we have done our best to cleanse ourselves and our homes, we know that all our efforts cannot lead to perfection. Some *hametz* will remain, hidden, out of sight, but there nonetheless. The best we can do is acknowledge the valuelessness of it ("let it be as the dust of the earth"), and ask God's help in making sure it has no dominion over our lives. There should be no guilt here. We have truly done our best. So much of our lives is just this way. We strive for perfection but we need to know when to give it a rest. As serious as this business of getting rid of the *hametz* is, we reach a point when we have to stop and move on to the next moment, the next task. This prayer allows us to do just that. We need such a prayer for all the tasks of our lives.

Acknowledge that you have done your best. Tell God you really tried. Ask God's help in recognizing that what is still left shall not control you or run your life.

PESACH AND THE COUNTING OF THE OMER

﹏

Passover celebrates birth—the birth of the earth through spring and the birth of the Jewish people through the exodus from Egypt and slavery. We pass through the birth waters of the parting Sea of Reeds and emerge on the other side, ready to begin our lives anew. The two types of renewal are both represented on the seder plate.

The fifty-day period (seven weeks plus one day) between Pesach and Shavuot is known as the counting of the Omer. It has both agricultural significance (waiting for the first crops) and historical/spiritual significance (waiting for the revelation of Torah at Mount Sinai). These next seven meditation themes are designed to move us from the escape out of slavery to the experience of Sinai.

meditations
FAITH AND COURAGE

The whole world is a very narrow bridge, but the essential thing is not to be at all afraid.

— REBBE NACHMAN OF BRATZLAV

We cannot change the reality of the world, only our response to it. And sometimes that world seems to be against us, limiting our lives. The Hebrew for Egypt is *Mitzrayim*. It comes from the root, *tzar*, which literally means "narrow/tight/constricted." (The Yiddish word *tzuris*/troubles is related). Egypt was a place that constricted our people, enslaving us. We had to leave that narrow place in order to become fully ourselves.

Perhaps this is a time in your life when you feel particularly limited by your choices. Perhaps you can remember another time the world seemed to be closing in on you. What are you afraid of? How can you get across that narrow bridge? Today, take your first step.

Therefore we pray to You instead, O God, for strength, determination, and willpower, to do what we can, to do what we must . . .

— RABBI JACK RIEMER

We spend a lot of time praying for and doing things we want to do, or what others want us to do. There is nothing wrong with this. But there is a tendency to mistake our wants for our needs, and to think of God as some cosmic dispensing machine. And when we do not get what we want, we throw a tantrum, withdrawing our belief, holding the relationship hostage. Most of us want a lot more than we need—not only to survive, but to be happy. God is here to help us with those needs. With our wants, we are on our own.

What is it that you *need* to do, today, this week, this lifetime? Set some realistic goals starting just with today. Ask for God's help in getting you there.

Courage is not the absence of fear; it is the making of action in spite of fear, the moving out against the resistance engendered by fear into the unknown and into the future.

— M. SCOTT PECK

There is nothing wrong with being afraid. In fact, sometimes, fear is absolutely the correct response to a situation, that which keeps us safe from harm. Fear can protect us, caution us against unnecessary risk, help us to measure our steps. Fear can be our ally. It will be present in times of danger. But fear can also get in our way, preventing us from doing what we must. We need always to recognize our fears, and then take them with us on our way.

Consider a time when your fear prevented you from taking action. Do you remember what it was you were afraid of? How might it have been different? What actions are you delaying now because of your fears? What can you do today to move out into the future?

Money lost, nothing lost. Courage lost, everything lost.
— YIDDISH FOLK SAYING

We spend much of our energy acquiring and spending and protecting our material well-being. Judaism does not demean the material world, for it, too, is a potential path to God. Wealth is not something to be despised or spurned. A rich person is no further from God than a poor one. It is how we use our material possessions that is the determining factor in whether it is a positive or a negative in our lives. Anything, any act, can be sanctified or made holy. But many of us are out of balance. We have forgotten that money is here to serve us, and to help us serve others, and not the other way around.

What if you lost "everything"? What would really change? What would be different? Would you be different?

We cannot banish dangers, but we can banish fears. We must not demean life by standing in awe of death.
— DAVID SARNOFF

Danger is real. It is part of our lives and our world. And we have learned to be cautious. But we sometimes think that our society and our time is more dangerous than any other. This is our fear talking. And the ultimate fear that many of us carry around is death itself. Not only our own, but that of the ones we love. As Jews we do not celebrate death; rather, we recognize it as a great sadness, the loss of a loved one. We tear our clothes, cry out in anguish, and grieve. And then we get back to the business of living, knowing that the one we love is always with us, that the spirit, which is the life force itself, can never die.

How much power over your life do you give death? How is (the fear of) death diminishing your life right now?

God is with me, I shall not fear.
— ADON OLAM, DAILY SIDDUR

Imagine God at your side, throughout the day. God is always there. Where else can the Eternal Ever-Present One be? Though at times we feel God's absence, we can always invite God to be with us. This is the promise of *shechinah,* the indwelling immanence of the One. Wherever we have gone—and we Jews have gone everywhere—God's presence has gone with us. And with God at our side, we have not been afraid. It is no different today, if only we would invite God into our lives. To the question "Where is God?" Levi Yitzhak of Berdichev answered, "Wherever we invite God in."

Try it. Invite God to be with you. Today. And every day.

❧ ❧ ❧

meditations
CHANGE/NEW REALITIES

One who resists the wave is swept away, but one who bends before it abides.

— GENESIS RABBAH 44:1

We are often told that what has kept Judaism alive is its continuity with the past. But this is only half the truth. We are actually one of the great assimilators in the history of the world, putting a Jewish slant on ideas, practices, even foods that we have borrowed from surrounding or host cultures. What we call Jewish often has its origins in the host culture of that time. Centuries later, we have forgotten those origins, and think of our current praxis as truly authentic. We need to remember that our people have lived just about everywhere and that in each of those places, whenever we were permitted to do so, we have mixed with and become part of the culture. We have influenced it, and it has influenced us as well.

What is it that you are resisting in your own life? How can you bend with it and make it uniquely your own?

This is also for the good.
— RABBI GAM ZU, TALMUD

We have probably all experienced some changes that deny the truth of this statement. Sometimes it appears that our lives may have gotten worse because of change. Yet the reality of the universe is that change is the only constant. Nothing can ever be the same. Even the cells in our bodies are continually dying and being replaced. So how do I begin to say, "Change is good"? How do I accept that each change—and change is inevitable—is also good? Perhaps in ways that I do not understand at this moment, but good, nevertheless.

Examine those elements in your life that have changed "for the worse." With each one, can you see any goodness that may have (or may still) come from it as well?

Restriction by others chains the mind; by oneself, paralyzes it.
— LUDWIG BORNE

We have little or no control over the restrictions others place on us. They can slow us down; they can even stop us from time to time. We can attempt to limit these restrictions, but cannot eliminate them completely. What we can do is not allow them to take over our lives. We do not have to give them that much power.

However, the restrictions we place on ourselves are the most insidious of all. Since they come from within, only internal change, changing the very way we think, can make an impact. So, what are the forces that are slowing you down? Are there any ways you can break these "chains"? Where are you "paralyzed" right now? What are you willing to do to overcome those self-limitations? What is holding you back from doing so—today?

We must implant firmly in our hearts the understanding that creation is a continuous process.
— MENACHEM BEN MOSES HABAVLI

In our daily liturgy, we thank God for "having created" the universe. But, while you never see it that way, the Hebrew verb should properly be translated to read that God "is creating" the universe. At every moment of every day, life—including our own—is being created. Nothing is static. Yet we often treat the world and those in it as if they are in stasis.

As you go through your day today, consider that everything is in process, which means that anything is possible.

Whoever would change people must change the conditions of their lives.

— THEODOR HERZL

Change does not occur in a vacuum. All things and all people are interconnected. We sometimes demand change of others, but are unwilling to change ourselves or to give of ourselves in order to facilitate such changes. We sometimes expect change of ourselves, but are unwilling or unable to change the very situation that led to our being stuck in the first place.

What are the changes you would like to see in yourself? In others? In our world? How could you help to create an environment in which such changes would be possible?

Today is merely a bridge to tomorrow.

— FRANZ ROSENZWEIG

Some will read this quote and think, "Today does not matter, it only gets me to the next day." But that, I think, is a misreading. Today is all I have. No one knows what tomorrow may bring or even if there will be a tomorrow. But we do need to put today in some kind of healthy perspective. Some of us are living our lives as if we must have it all now. We have forgotten how to wait, how to delay gratification. And in the process, we are missing out on so much that surrounds us, that is at our very fingertips.

Tomorrow reminds us that life does indeed go on, that there will be new insights and new possibilities. Tomorrow reminds us to slow down and leave something for the next day.

What is it that you are killing yourself to get accomplished today that can really wait until tomorrow? What is the tomorrow you would like to create through your actions today?

meditations

FREEDOM

I have set before you life and death, blessing or curse; choose life, therefore, that you and your descendants may live—by loving Adonai your God, listening to God's voice, clinging to the One who is your life and the length of your days.

— DEUTERONOMY 30:9–10

In the Reform movement, we read this section of the Torah on the morning of Yom Kippur. It reminds us that in order to live (not merely exist), our lives need to be bound up with God, and God's purpose. Such a decision is our choice; it can only be made by one who is free. Judaism is predicated on freedom. We can choose or reject God only because we have the freedom to do so. To choose God, our Torah text tells us, is to choose a life of value and meaning and blessing.

How are you choosing God in your life? Where are you resisting or keeping God out? Make two lists. For each place of resistance, what (if anything) are you willing to do to bring God in?

*Destiny and freedom are solemnly promised each to the other.
[But] only the one who makes freedom real to himself achieves
his destiny.*

— MARTIN BUBER

Each of us is here to fulfill a particular and unique task. We
spend much of our lives trying to figure out just what that is. As
ironic as it may sound, unless and until we realize our freedom, this
destiny will remain obscure or hidden. We must experience our
freedom, free from the habits that enslave us, in order to know
our true path in life. The Israelite slave who chose not to mark his
door with the blood of freedom remained behind in Egyptian
slavery, and did not achieve his destiny as a Jew.

What is your destiny? Which enslavements do you need to cast
off so that you can taste true freedom?

*For over a hundred years, a large part of the American people has
imagined that the virtual meaning of life lies in the acquisition of
ever-increasing status, income and authority, from which genuine
freedom is supposed to come . . . Yet we seem to be hovering
on the very brink of disaster.*

— ROBERT BELLAH

We have come to believe that freedom means doing whatever
you want. But that is not true freedom; it is anarchy. In order for
there to be true freedom, there must be limits. Without such limits,
we all lose our freedom. Torah is instruction in freedom with limits.
As a society, after decades of throwing off limits, we are now
realizing the pain of all that excess. And our great-grandchildren
will still be paying for it. We do not want to return to slavery, but
we cannot afford any more golden calves.

In what parts of your life are you out of control? What limits are
you willing to accept so that you can experience true freedom?

*The roads to freedom do not run through the lands out yonder,
rather through our inner selves.*

— ARTHUR SCHNITZLER

We think that freedom is just beyond our reach, in buying this,
going there, trying that. And so we run around, trying to purchase
it, experience it, find it. We blame our circumstances or our
partners or our children for tying us down, enslaving us, keeping us
from being free. Certainly, outside factors play a role. But the first
thing that our ancestors had to do to escape from Egyptian slavery
was tether a lamb and keep it on display for three days. The act
identified them as Israelites, separating them from those who would
remain behind. They had to free themselves, had to think about themselves as free, in order to be free. The work begins with the self.

What are you blaming for your lack of freedom? What movement within yourself are you willing to make in order to be free?

*God is responsible for having created a world in which we are
free to make history.*

— RABBI ELIEZER BERKOVITS

One of the questions I am frequently asked by children is, "Why
did God make bad people?" And my answer is invariably the same:
"God did not make bad people. God made people and gives them
the choice to be good or bad. God wants us to choose the good, but
we are free to choose the bad." And then I ask, "If you were God,
would you have made people and programmed them to be good
[this is the nineties—they understand computer talk] without
giving them choices?" Very rarely does a hand go up to say, "Yes."

God created a world in which we are free. Free will is a basic
reality of the universe as we Jews understand it. We are not bound
by fate or destiny or even our previous choices.

Think about your life as a history. What have been the defining moments up to now? Envision your future as a time line stretching out beyond today. What would you like to see recorded on that blank space?

Freedom is an unremitting endeavor, never a final achievement.
— FELIX FRANKFURTER

Each and every Pesach we are required to read the Haggadah as if we too were being freed from Egypt. Did you ever wonder why that is so? After all, most of us were born in freedom and have never tasted the misery of slavery. But the Haggadah wants us to pretend that this is not a past event that happened to our ancestors four thousand years ago, but that it is happening to us, each and every year. Thus our tradition teaches us that freedom is not something that is gained once and forever; rather, it is something that must be earned and renewed, safeguarded and cherished.

How are you earning your freedom today? What are you doing to protect it?

meditations

RESPONSIBILITY

Responsible consists of two words—"response" and "able." To be responsible means that we are capable of responding, to others and their needs.

— TOM DALY

We tend to think of responsibility as a burden, something that weighs us down. Something that means we are always doing for others, and we never get to do what we want. We have equated responsibility with obligation, and so we run away from it. Another way to look at it, though, is as a positive characteristic, a quality that deepens us as human beings. A quality that adds texture and meaning to our lives.

To whom are you "response able"? Who are the people in your life to whom you are not? Why is that? What is preventing you from becoming "response able" to each person you meet?

A man in a boat began to bore a hole under his seat. When his fellow passengers asked him what he was doing, he answered: What do you care? Am I not boring under my own seat?
— LEVITICUS RABBAH

We have practically been weaned on the credo, "So long as what I do is not hurting anyone else . . ." But we have come to see that there is no such thing as an isolated, atomistic self. The American image of the cowboy riding off by himself into the sunset may work fine in the movies, but it is not real. All of us are connected, one to the other. And our actions inevitably affect other people as well. Many of us are so focused on ourselves that we don't even realize the impact we have on those around us, especially those we love.

What holes have you been boring in your life, thinking, "It's only *my* seat"? Are you willing to take a look at how they are affecting the lives of others, especially the ones you love?

Self-achieved submission is a marker of the true hero.
— JOSEPH CAMPBELL

We live in a culture of narcissism, in which fulfilling our ever-changing and expanding list of wants has become the primary goal of life. Our insatiable appetites have created a society where short-term, immediate gratification, enormous debt, and moral decay are the norm. Going entirely in the opposite direction—practicing ascetic denial—is not the answer either (according to Jewish tradition). Perhaps we can consider the middle path. Judaism has always preferred the path of sanctification. We take the stuff of this world—money, food, sex, etc.—limit our appetites, and turn our material actions into holy ones. It is the creation of these limits that is so lacking in our lives and in our world.

Where are you out of control? Where do you need to cut back? Where do you need to give in to the will/needs of another? Take a single step in that direction. And then take another.

Do not ask God what you want; ask God what the Holy One wants for you.

— CHOFETZ CHAIM

Those of us who were around in the 1960s will hear an echo of President Kennedy's famous inaugural address in this nineteenth-century statement by the Chofetz Chaim. We know what we want. We are experts at it. And we spend so much of our lives getting it, some of us openly, others in secret. There is no shame in having wants. And there is no problem with working hard to acquire or achieve them. It is merely a matter of balance and control—of considering not only what we want, but what God wants for us. This is the beginning of responsibility.

What is it that God wants for you? What is it that God expects? Today, ask God what His/Her will is for you. Say, "God, show me Your will for me and give me the courage and strength to carry it out." Say it today and every day. And listen/watch carefully for God's response. This is a prayer God always answers in time.

Bars don't corrupt good men and temples don't transform bad ones.

— YIDDISH FOLK SAYING

My youngest son is fond of saying, "It's none of my fault!" after every accident and misdeed. It has become a kind of family joke. The issue, though, for all of us, is not one of blame and fault. Cause and effect may work well in a laboratory experiment, but real life is more complicated than that. The truth is, we are responsible for all that befalls us. We got us to where we are. Sure, others contributed—pushed, prodded, or persuaded us to do or choose certain deeds or paths. But we are ultimately responsible. And we will have to live with the consequences.

What failure, what loss are you blaming on somebody else? What action that went undone or goal not attained? What unrealized potential? Are you ready to let go of all the excuses and take ownership of your own life?

It is not incumbent upon you to complete the work. But neither are you free from doing what you can.

— PIRKE AVOT 2:21

My problem with all the self-help literature is that it lays everything at the doorstep of the individual. If you have the right diet, the right attitude, the right workout . . . then you can do anything and everything; you can have it all and always be happy. Yes, we have a great deal of power. No, we cannot do it all, not by ourselves. The above quote from Pirke Avot goes on to say, "The day is short and the Master of the house is waiting . . ." So what are you waiting for? What work have you been putting off because it feels so overwhelming, because you cannot possibly complete it? Get started right now, today. You do not have to do it all. Invite others to help. Ask God, too.

~~ ~~ ~~

meditations
COMMITMENT

I will betroth you to Me forever; I will betroth you to Me in righteousness and justice, in love and compassion; I will betroth you to Me in faithfulness, and you will know Adonai.
— HOSEA 2:21 (said while winding *tefillin* around one's fingers)

The prophet depicts the relationship between God and the Jewish people as a marriage which has no possibility of divorce. Lots of tumult, plenty of fighting, a falling-out or two along the way, some temporary separation, but no permanent divorce. It is a marriage made up of the purest qualities, which leads to a complete knowing of one another. Recognizing our responsibilities can lead us (if we do not falter) to the next stage of the relationship—commitment. We are out there in the wilderness of our journey, heading toward our highest self. There is no turning back.

What are the things and who are the people to whom you are really committed? Where are you holding back from true commitment? What will it take to get you there?

Judaism has a central, unique and tremendous idea that is utterly original—the idea that God and humans are partners in the world and that, for the realization of God's plan and the complete articulation of this plan upon earth, God needs a committed, dedicated group of men and women.
— THEODORE GASTER

We are God's partners. God's hands and feet. The role of the Jew, the task for which we are chosen, is to carry out God's will on earth. To make God known through the living of a life of good deeds, selflessness, *mitzvah*. This does not make us any better than anyone else, just different in this respect. Others may have other tasks, connected to God in their own way; that is not for me to say. My job is to be the best partner I possibly can be.

Your doing the workout is one act of dedication and commitment. What else will you do today that will demonstrate your partnership with God? Ask yourself, in every task you undertake, "Am I being a good partner by doing _____ ?"

Blessed is the one who keeps the foundation of the ancestors.
— II ENOCH 52:9

The Judaism we live today is different from the one of the Torah, different from even that of a generation ago. In fact, it is Judaism's ability to change and adapt to new realities that has kept it alive and vital. Nevertheless, there are core values that form its "foundation" that cannot and do not change.

What do you consider the "foundation" of Judaism? What is something you inherited from your parents or grandparents that you keep within yourself?

Religion will not come to our aid the moment we call; it must be loved and cherished at all times if it is to prove our true friend in need.
— GUSTAVE GOTTHEIL

So many of us want religion to "work" whenever we choose to pull it off some dusty shelf; we get angry or disappointed when it does not. While there are spontaneous moments in which we sense

God's transcendent reality and our connection to all of creation, true spirituality is a discipline. It takes work. And so we work out, praying for the insight/awareness to hear God's word, to see His/Her presence in our lives.

What is it that you love about Judaism? How do you cherish it? Share it with someone you know.

I call heaven and earth to serve as witnesses this day that I have set before you life and death, blessing or curse; choose life, therefore, that you and your descendants may live . . .

— DEUTERONOMY 30:19

The choice is always ours. A life of blessing with God, or a life of death, without. A life of death? While the Torah may be speaking literally of physical mortality, we have learned that there are existences in which one may be physically alive, doing quite well in fact, while the spirit is dead inside. That is what I call a life of death. We all know such people. Perhaps we once existed in that lifeless way ourselves—and then, for some reason we do not know, a spark was kindled. That spark can become a flame, and we can come to life. Just as you are attempting to do right now.

The choice is ours and we need to choose life, a life with God. It is not so difficult, is it? How will you demonstrate your commitment to this choice today?

To be is to stand for.

— RABBI ABRAHAM JOSHUA HESCHEL

It comes down to that. Not only are our lives given shape and meaning by the things for which we stand; rather, the very task of being human is about standing for. That is how our humanity is determined. That is how we become truly human. By standing for. That is the purest definition of commitment I know.

If someone were to look at your life, what would they say you stood for? What would you want them to say? Do you demonstrate that with your commitment? Are you sure?

meditations
COVENANT

A person's real work in this world is the work of the Blessed Holy One.

— RABBI ELAZAR, IN THE ZOHAR

We identify ourselves as doctors, homemakers, lawyers, teachers. . . . But as Jews, our one and only true occupation is "partner with God." That is the meaning of the word "covenant." Beginning with Abraham and Sarah, we have all entered into a relationship that is both sacred and eternal. Each of us is given a myriad of opportunities each and every day to do God's work in this world. From feeding the hungry to dealing honestly in business, from doing this workout to driving a little more courteously this morning . . . there are no actions, no words that cannot be lifted up to God.

As you go through your day, be aware of the ways in which you are doing God's work.

"You are My witnesses that I am God" (Isaiah 43:12). When you are My witnesses, I am God; when you are not My witnesses, I am, as it were, not God.

— MIDRASH TEHILLIM 123:2

What chutzpah! God needs us to be God? Yet, that is what we say. We are important. We are necessary. What we do matters. It is our witnessing, by word and deed, that makes God's presence manifest in the world. In part, this is what sustained our people through the horrors of exile and persecution. "They" despised us. But we knew who we were and the importance of our mission. Whether it was self-imposed or God's will, who knows? But we are still here. Still challenged to witness.

Be a witness for God today. Remember, it can be with your words or your actions. They both can speak loudly.

You shall further instruct the Israelites to bring clear oil of beaten olives to maintain an Eternal light.

— EXODUS 27:20

The building of the Tabernacle, the physical space for worship of God, was brought about by voluntary contributions. But the *Ner Tamid,* the Eternal Light, was the equal responsibility of every Jew. Every Jew had the responsibility of bringing pure oil to be used in this special lamp. In our own time, this light, representing God's continuous presence in our lives, is kept burning through our faithful actions.

How will you keep the light burning today?

And God said to Israel, "My beloved children, am I in want of anything that I should request it of you? But what I ask of you is that you should love, honor, and respect one another."

— SEDER ELIYAHU RABBAH 26

It comes down to this: Our ultimate responsibility is to care for one another, to "love thy neighbor." And interestingly enough, our treatment of one another is totally beyond God's control. The true measure of our humanity, and thus our covenantal loyalty, will be made manifest by the way in which we take care of one another. That is the only thing God wants from us—the only thing God cannot do for us.

Write the words down where you can see them today—"love," "honor," "respect." Make that the prism through which you evaluate all your behavior.

The recognition of a person's innate dignity as God's coworker is basic to a proper understanding of one's nature, as manifested in one's creative ability, one's moral responsibility, and one's untapped potentialities.

— ROBERT GORDIS

It is not all output, not all what we do for others. Being in covenant with God also nourishes and feeds us. It brings us to our full humanity. We have been led to believe that life with God will diminish us, cut us off from what we really want to do. In fact, just the opposite is true. It is through our partnering with the One before Whom all is known that we get to know and realize who and what we are.

Today, ask God to help you to reach your untapped potential. It is what God wants as well.

A person's good deeds are used by God as seeds for planting trees in the Garden of Eden; thus, each person creates his/her own Paradise.

— DOV BAER, THE MAGGID OF MEZERITZ

There are mysteries of the universe that, in our human limitation, we can never understand. One such mystery is the very notion of the covenant itself. Why would the Creator of All need a not-

so-very-loyal, stiff-necked band of whining complainers as a partner? It defies our understanding. Yet here we are, four millennia
later, holding fast—not always doing the best job of it, but hanging
in there nevertheless. And it is through our acts of loyalty, large and
small—a mezuzah on our house, the *bris* of a child, a late night
meeting at the temple, a trip to Israel—that the very trees of
Paradise are being planted.

Celebrate the mystery. Plant another tree, today. Create your
own paradise.

∿   ∿   ∿

meditations
REVELATION

*The counting from Passover to Shavuot is carried out as is done
by the one who waits for the coming of the one he loves best,
counting the days, even the hours until the arrival.*
— MOSES MAIMONIDES (RAMBAM)

Our tradition marks a seven-week period of counting from
Passover to Shavuot, linking the two holy days that we call the
Omer. In ancient times, the people brought an omer of wheat to the
Temple in Jerusalem as a way of thanking God for this first sign of
the good harvest to come. Later, our rabbis understood the
revelation of Shavuot as the fulfillment of the freedom we gained at
Passover. The Haggadah asked us to be slaves. Shavuot asks us to
gather at our synagogues to receive the revelation of Torah.

Make final preparations to receive the Torah. Plan out where
you will be, what clothes you will wear, the dinner you will eat and
with whom. Six weeks ago you were a slave in Egypt. One more
week and you will taste the only true freedom—the freedom of
God's revelation.

Only in moments when we are able to share in the spirit of awe that fills the world are we able to understand what happened to Israel at Sinai. Revelation means that the thick silence which fills the endless distance between God and the human being was pierced.

— RABBI ABRAHAM JOSHUA HESCHEL

It is so difficult to understand revelation. Perhaps it simply must be experienced, rather than understood. Think of moments in which you truly felt awestruck at the wonder that is life. Perhaps in those moments you felt a sense of your greatness and your smallness, connected to all that ever was and all that ever will be. Perhaps in those moments you felt that you just knew, that everything seemed to make sense, that everything had purpose and meaning. That was revelation. At Sinai, our entire people felt that way for a moment. Shared by everyone, it transformed us, shaped us, made us a people.

The promise of Sinai is that revelation is ongoing and continuous, available to each and every one of us at any moment. Listen. Watch. Get ready.

Revelation is the silent, imperceptible manifestation of God in history. It is the still, small voice; it is the inevitability, the regularity of nature.

— HERBERT LOEWE

We also embrace the possibility that revelation doesn't require loud noises, smoking mountains, or incredible awe. Revelation is part of us, part of nature, part of history. As Jews we are challenged to believe that God cares about us and so takes part in our day-to-day lives. God is not out there, somewhere, but right here, inside of us, closer than the air we breathe.

Sit quietly for a moment. Take a deep breath, inhaling through your nose and exhaling through your mouth. Really let go of that breath. Keep breathing deeply. You might want to close your eyes. That *neshama*/breath, which is life, is also God. God out there. God in here. Listen for the voice inside yourself. That, too, is revelation.

And Adonai said to Moses, "Go to the people and sanctify them today and tomorrow, and let them wash their garments, and be ready for the third day . . ."

— EXODUS 19:10–11

We sometimes think that being holy is some big deal that only specially designated people can even attempt to achieve. But the Torah tells us that holiness can be found in something as simple as washing our clothes, lighting a candle, drinking a glass of wine. Washing is a symbol of purification, and a part of many traditional Jewish rituals (as well as the rituals of other religious groups). Why? Because water is life.

Think up some simple ritual that you can do. It could be washing your clothes, taking a bath, getting your nails done, or anything else that helps you feel a separation, a change, different somehow. Being holy or sanctified, *kadosh,* is about such moments of separation and change. Do *your* ritual in preparation for Shavuot. Let it begin to bring you a sense of sanctity and holiness.

Every day there is a heavenly voice that emanates from the mountain of Sinai, but we are so wrapped up in ourselves that we fail to listen.

— AUTHOR UNKNOWN

We are busy. We run from activity to activity, trying to be good mothers and fathers, competent professionals, attentive children, empathic friends. We, who were supposed to have so much leisure and free time, who were supposed to be in control of our lives and our schedules, find ourselves barely able to keep up with it all. Forget about stopping to smell the roses—we didn't even see them there at the side of the road! How did it get so crazy?

The voice is still calling us. It is not too late to listen. All we have to do is stop for a while. It will all be there waiting for us when we get back. Pay attention. Spend some time listening today. Listen to your heart beating. Listen to your breath going in and out. What is it that you hear?

The giving of the Torah happened at one specified time, but the receiving of Torah happens all the time, in every generation.
— THE GERER REBBE

Everything you have done these past seven weeks has been leading you to tomorrow, to Shavuot. When you stand at Shavuot services, hearing the Ten Commandments read, you are to imagine yourself standing at Mount Sinai, hearing them for the first time. This is not something you can do today. Today you can only get ready to be there tomorrow. Tomorrow you can accept that God is the commander, that God is in control, and that you are subject to God's will.

Ask God's help in getting you ready. Ask God to soften your heart, to sharpen your hearing, to strengthen your resolve, so that you can receive God's Torah. Then every day will be Shavuot. And every place, Sinai.

SHAVUOT

Shavuot is a time of adolescence and instruction. That is why we receive the Torah. It will become our guide for the journey through the wilderness, which is the path of each of our lives. We all must enter the wilderness in order to come to adult maturity. On Shavuot we give up our first fruits. Like our first love, we will always remember this experience, even if the details get a bit blurry.

meditations
TORAH

It is a tree of life to them that hold fast to it . . . draw us close unto You, Adonai, and we will return, renew our days as of old.
— PRAYER UPON RETURNING THE TORAH TO THE ARK

Once, a very long time ago, at a mountaintop we call Sinai, our people encountered God, and the world has never been the same. Our people's response then was "*na'aseh v'nishmah*/we will do, and then we will understand." First we will do, then understand. First we will create the relationship and then afterward try to figure out what it means. And so each of us has the same opportunity to respond. What will our response be? Will we stand on the side, like a spectator, or will we grab on tight to this Torah which has always been ours?

There are signs all around us that people are ready to receive the Torah. There are many new books on the market, recasting the old tales into a modern sensibility. Torah study classes and Bible groups abound. What is keeping you from joining one if you haven't yet? Are you ready to "hold fast" to the Torah? Ask God to draw you closer.

Not only does every synagogue contain this book, it is primarily by virtue of its presence, together with that of a congregation, that a synagogue is a synagogue . . . And here, in the role assigned to a book, we have that clue to the spirit and structure of Judaism . . .

— RABBI MILTON STEINBERG

We have been called "The People of the Book," and wherever we have gone (and we have gone everywhere) the Book has come along with us. It has been carried out of burning buildings in our people's darkest moments; it has been danced with, lifting us up, at our people's greatest joys. More than anything else, Torah defines who and what we are. It gives shape and texture to the Jewish enterprise. Through our struggle with a text—reading and rereading it each year, poring over its meaning, challenging it as it challenges us—we begin to understand what it means to be a Jew.

It can begin very simply, without much investment. Buy a *chumash* or Torah text with commentary. Find a Jewish calendar that lists the weekly Torah portion. (It is usually written in the "Saturday" box.) Assign a designated time each week in your personal calendar to read/study as much of that week's portion as you can. Don't worry about what you don't get to—there is always next year.

Imagine your weekly schedule. Now imagine it again with Torah study slotted in.

Said Rabbi Yohanan, "His delight and trust in me rose up so strongly in Him that He drew out the Torah for me as a mother draws out her breast for her child."

— PESIKTA D'RAV KAHANA

We think of thunder and lightning, of smoking mountains and fiery skies. But perhaps it is as natural and quiet as a mother nursing her child. God, the mother, giving life-sustaining milk to her baby. As simple and as beautiful as that.

How many of us have sought the truth in exotic experiences? How far have we traveled to find answers, seeking teachers to tell us what we already knew deep inside ourselves? And all the while God, who delights in us, was waiting to give it freely, and in love.

Can you imagine yourself as a baby drinking deeply from your mother's milk? Can you "taste" the Torah coursing through your body, giving you life and strength, enabling you to grow?

We study the Torah not to learn more about it; but to learn more about ourselves.

— RABBI KERRY OLITZKY

The Torah is a mirror. A clear and perfect mirror. And if we are willing to look into it with open eyes, we may just get a glimpse of ourselves. That is why there are no perfect people in its pages. To remind us that we, too, do not have to be perfect. We come with our flaws and our limitations, our wounds and our scars. It is okay. Torah invites us to look and to accept, to grow and to change. It is not a utopian worldview. No fantasy or flights of fancy. It is about real people living real lives with real problems doing the best they can. Sometimes succeeding, sometimes failing—just like us. They did not teach it to us this way in religious school. Forget about religious school. Torah is about us, you and me. That is its challenge and its promise.

What is it that you want to learn about yourself? Write your questions down. Let the Torah answer them through your study of its words.

The Torah is like one of those romantic historical novels, a love story between God and the Jewish people, complete with moments of passion and at-oneness, lots of fights and crises, with Moses the marriage therapist working to keep the partners together.

— Ratbal

For those of us who grew up thinking the Torah had to be true, with "true" meaning that it really happened that way, reimagining the Torah in this way can be quite confrontational. But something can be true even if it did not happen, because of the truth it contains, and the truth it teaches us. The truth of the Torah goes far beyond its historical accuracy. It even goes beyond its authorship. Think of your and God's relationship as that of two lovers. Have you been a good partner? What about lately? Do you call? Write love letters? Do you do those little things that remind our loved ones that we still care? Or has the relationship fallen into dull routine? Or equally as bad, have you become estranged from one another? Is it time for some counseling? Perhaps your rabbi could help.

I will teach you the best way to say Torah. You must cease to be aware of yourselves. You must be nothing but an ear that hears what the universe is saying within you. The moment you start hearing what you yourself are saying, you must stop.

— Ten Rungs, Martin Buber

We go looking all around the world trying to find it when all along it is inside of us, each and every one of us. And the way to access it is by becoming a "listening," a listening for the universe which speaks within us. The difficult part is shutting off all the noise. And that is what meditation is really all about. Tuning out the noise so that we can hear what the universe is saying.

There are a number of methods for doing so—repetition of a sound or word (mantra), visualization of a design or element in nature, focusing on breathing, light or color imaging, and chanting are the best known. Some are associated with different postures. Each has its own proponents but they are all effective. They all aim at the same goal. You just have to experiment and find the one that works best for you. And keep listening.

What is the "Torah" within you? Can you hear it? Are you listening?

SUMMER

You shall be holy, for I the Lord am holy.
—LEVITICUS 19:2

"All religions are basically the same. They try to get you to be a good person. Right?" Wrong. The goal of Judaism is holiness, not goodness. We are to strive to be holy, each and every one of us (not just the rabbis), in imitation of God, who is also holy. Goodness might be a start, but it is not good enough. Holiness asks us to strive for something more, something greater. It asks us to be set apart, to be unique, special, different. As much as anything else, it is the foundation of Judaism. The idea of the holiness of an entire people is without parallel in any religious system. We are to be a nation of priests with each home a *mikdash m'at*/small sanctuary, with each table its own altar. No one can do this work for us. No one has to.

How do you strive for holiness in your own life?

Holiness should be built on a foundation of the everyday and mundane.
—RAV KOOK

When we hear the word "holy" we often think of someone who has chosen a life based on ascetic withdrawal from society and all earthly pleasures. And certainly there are religious systems which ask their adherents and especially their leaders to accept vows of poverty and/or celibacy. There are religious approaches that require leaders to live communally, free of the burden that comes along with ownership of property or possessions. While we understand the power of such an approach, it is not Jewish. Judaism asks for no such withdrawal from the world of the everyday. In fact, it is just the opposite. It is only through the world of the everyday, by being a "householder" and holding down a job, that one can achieve a true measure of holiness.

The path of Judaism is to sanctify the mundane, to raise it up to the level of holiness, to turn every action into a holy act. By being fair and honest in our business dealings, by blessing the food we eat, by sharing of our means with those who have none, we begin to live a life of holiness, a life sanctified to God.

Think of the day that lies ahead of you today. What actions will you take that could be considered holy? What are some ways you can sanctify the things you do each day?

Holiness is true community with God, and true community with human beings, both in one.

— MARTIN BUBER

Again, Judaism defies our usual expectation. We think of the holy man or woman as one who is separated from the world, which serves to corrupt us. It is only at the top of the mountain, away from human habitation, we believe, that we can commune with God. But in fact, while we may seek the mountaintop from time to time, it is only down at the bottom that we can live the life of holiness. We do not achieve oneness with God without others. Nor can we achieve oneness with others without God. Holiness is the recognition that they are one and the same. Holiness requires the individual to be part of the community.

Is there a balance in your life? Or are you trying to find holiness without community? Holiness without God? Give thanks for the balance if it exists. Keep looking if it does not, or start looking for it if you never have.

If one sanctifies her/himself a little, s/he will be sanctified a great deal.

—TALMUD, YOMA 39A

It begins as service, but ends up as reward. It begins with us making the effort, doing the work, but ends up with our receiving more than we gave. We do not have to do it all. Just a little. I am not sure how this works, but I have seen it so many times that I am convinced it works just this way. It is as if once we have created a space for holiness in our lives, nothing unholy can exist there any longer. And the more space we create, the more holiness there is. Sanctified action provides us with a certain clarity by which we can detect and then reject all that would bring the unholy back into our presence. Sanctified action raises the stakes, which are our lives, and lifts us and all that we do to a higher plain of holiness. This is the blueprint behind the idea of a Holy Land—a place in which all actions aim at holiness, a place in which even God can dwell. There is something very powerful, even life-transforming, in taking these steps toward holiness. What are some little steps that you can take today?

The one who has not tasted sin is not qualified for holiness.

—JACOB KLATZKIN

We need to be disabused of the notion that holy equals perfect, or that only "little angels" can arrive at any meaningful level of holiness. Not only is this untrue, but the opposite is the case. It is through our experience with sin (i.e., moving away from God and God's will for us) that we can apprehend or approach the holy. Sin can be our entry card, the price of admission. Sin provides us with perspective, a distance from which to gaze on and appreciate the holy. Sin moves us away so that we know how to get back. It helps us to realize our humanity, to put some humility into all our efforts. God save us from those who claim never to have sinned, who present themselves as always perfect.

Stop waiting to be perfect. Stop beating yourself up with all that you have done to separate yourself from a life of holiness, or all that you have failed to do in order to journey there. Instead think of those things as qualifying actions. All that got you to the starting gate. Now begin. Now continue.

Whatever God has created has a spark of holiness in it.
> — BA'AL SHEM TOV

How can this be? There is so much evil and ugliness in our world. How can they contain a spark of holiness? Whatever God has created—you and me, the natural forces of the universe, the animals and plants—has a spark of holiness in it. And one of our jobs, as Jews and as children of God, is to find and release that spark, to fan it into a flame, a flame that will warm and heal our world. It is there. We may not see it at first glance. But God does not create anything without attaching a signature. And that signature is the spark of holiness.

At *havdallah,* when we say farewell to our Shabbat day of holiness, we hold our fingers up to the light of the candle in order to see the spark shining in our fingertips. It reminds us that the spark is there, as it is in every human being. It reminds us to treat each person with the knowledge that s/he contains that spark—the spark of holiness. What do you do to remind yourself that all of creation holds the spark? What are you doing to fan the sparks into a flame? What can you do?

❧   ❧   ❧

meditations
MYSTERY

The illusion of total intelligibility, the indifference to the mystery
that is everywhere, the foolishness of ultimate self-reliance are
serious obstacles on the way. It is in moments of our being faced
with the mystery of living and dying, of knowing and not
knowing, of love and the inability to love—that we pray, that we
address ourselves to the One who is beyond the mystery.
— RABBI ABRAHAM JOSHUA HESCHEL

Modernity has taught us some wonderful lessons about things like the dignity of the individual regardless of race, creed, or color, the full equality of men and women, and the system of democracy by which we govern our communal lives. But we are now coming to realize it has also taught us lessons that block us from appreciating some of the ultimate truths of the universe. We grew up thinking that if we just searched long and hard enough, we could solve any mystery. We believed it was only our ignorance that stopped us and that ignorance was just a temporary condition, one that with enough learning and knowledge we could overcome.

We were wrong. There are mysteries that have no solutions. There are some things that simply remain unknown to us because they are unknowable. Life is not an Agatha Christie novel in which you know that if you just read long enough you will get to the answer. Mystery is part and parcel of life itself.

What are the things you are trying to "know"? Examine them. Can any of them be placed in the category of "mystery," simply unknowable? Are you ready to let go of the idea that you can comprehend/understand them? Why not?

The reason why we had to call it [transcendence] "mystery" con-
sisted ultimately in the fact that we experience it as that which
cannot be encompassed by a pre-apprehension which reaches
beyond it, and hence, it cannot be defined.

— FR. KARL RAHNER

God is ultimate mystery. The One that lies beyond all mysteries. Transcendence, that moment in which we touch or are touched by God, is also a mystery. We cannot anticipate it, nor can we define it. But we can (and do) experience it, often in ways that surprise us, catch us off guard, shake us to our core, fill us with a sense that all is good in life, that everything will turn out okay. It may have been when we saw our children being born, or that first day of spring after a dreary winter, or the call we made to a dying friend . . . We cannot define it. But we know it nevertheless.

Think of the moments in your life when you were touched in this way. You may have tried to hold on to them. You may have tried to describe them to someone else. When words failed you, were you tempted to dismiss the whole thing? But there are no words. There are just the experiences. Remember them now. Don't try to define anything. Just feel your connection to the transcendent mystery of the universe we call God.

If there is any miracle in the world, any mystery, it is individu-
ality.

— RABBI LEO BAECK

A *midrash* speaks of the difference between human creation and God's creation. With us, when we use a prototype, say a coin to make other coins, each of them is identical. But God used Adam and Eve to make each of us, and we are all unique. No two human beings are exactly alike, not even twins. And from what I can tell as a parent, it begins at birth. While nurture has something to do with it, each of my children were born with their own proclivities, their own personalities. That really is amazing. In fact, there is a blessing upon entering a room filled with people which thanks God for having made each of us different.

We spend much of our time trying to fit in, to be like everyone else. Wearing the right fashions, saying the right things. Today, think of what makes you uniquely you. Focus on your individuality. And give thanks for this mystery.

The most beautiful experience we can have is the mysterious.
— ALBERT EINSTEIN

My vision of the scientist is the one trying to unlock the mysteries of the universe. This is a scientist's passion—the search for truth, for knowledge, for control. And here comes Dr. Einstein to tell us that what is mysterious is also beautiful; that in fact, it is the most beautiful of all experiences we can have.

There is beauty in not knowing, in being awash in the mystery of being. Can you feel it? Can you let go long enough to experience mystery as beautiful, as nonthreatening, not scary? Can you allow yourself the abandonment that requires?

Lean back with your eyes closed, your arms opened wide. Be there with all of life's mysteries. Welcome them into your life

Who looks at these four things deserves not to have entered the world: what is above, what is below, what is in front, what is behind.
— TALMUD, HAGGIGAH 11A

When it came to the laws about gossip, the Chofetz Chaim said it would really be better if we never spoke about a third party. When I mention this to some people, they ask, "Then what would we talk about?!" If we did not look at what was above or below, in front or behind, what would we look at? And the answer to the two questions is the same. We would talk about/look at what is present, what is within. And this would raise the level, deepen the quality of all our conversations, all our searches.

It is probably impossible for most of us to stay so focused. Perhaps it is not even all that desirable. After all, our lives have been made so much better by all the discoveries in the world around us. Yet the challenge of the Talmud's statement remains. Can we stay focused in the present? Can we look within?

Try to be totally present in your meditation today. Forget about yesterday, forget about tomorrow. There is only now. There is only you. What do you feel? What is going on inside?

How God rules the universe . . . is a complete mystery.
— MOSES MAIMONIDES (RAMBAM)

On Sunday mornings, before religious school classes begin, I lead a worship service for kindergartners through second graders and their parents. In one part of the service I have the congregation ask "God questions." They range from "Who created God?" to "Why do skunks smell?" and everything in between. Children especially want to know how God does everything. "How did God create the universe? How did God create me?" "With words," I answer. And to many of their questions I find myself responding, "We just don't know."

Now while this satisfies most of the kids, and the majority of the adults as well, it doesn't always satisfy me. The truth is, we have so very little understanding of the way things really work, of the way God works. I have spent most of my life trying to figure myself out, making only limited progress. Imagine trying to figure God out! As the Zohar states, "It is all one mystery."

Contemplate the mystery without trying to figure it out. Let it be a mystery and be okay with that. Say it. "It is all one mystery, and that's okay."

~ ~ ~

meditations

Mitzvah/Commandment

It is built into the very definition and basic assumption of a mitzvah that it is the human response to the "Commanding Presence of God." That response is not, and cannot be, invariably the same.

— Rabbi Herman Schaalman

Judaism posits this. There is a Commander (God) and a commanded (us). This Commander has a will for us which we have called *mitzvah,* and which extends to every aspect of life. It is our task, first and foremost, to do God's will, to be *mitzvah* doers. But what is a *mitzvah*? We were taught it was a simple list of "thou shalts" and "thou shalt nots," but now we see it is more than that, much more. It is our existential response to the voice of God, which calls us still. It is our commitment to the historic relationship between God and the Jewish people. It is a personal act of devotion, performed "with all my heart, with all my soul, with all my might." Such doing can never be automatic and routine. Such doing must engage the totality of my being. There is no room for habit, or convention, or ceremony. *Mitzvah* is the free-will act of a liberated person, an individual act called forth at any moment. That is why we had to leave the bondage of Egypt in order to become (truly and fully) the Jewish people.

What is the *mitzvah* calling you? How will you respond?

83　　　　　　THE BUSY SOUL

The Ten Commandments assert that the force in the making of a civilized people is God's will, and that without God's will, there is formlessness and void.

— MAURICE SAMUEL

It begins with freedom. But freedom without control is chaos, subject to every whim. On the other hand, control without freedom is tyranny. We live in a time in which many of our friends, frightened by freedom and disappointed by modernity, subject themselves to human authorities (in the name of God) who make it easy for them, who tell them what to do, how to live their lives. We want something between these two extremes.

Mitzvah represents God's will for us, which we must strive to understand and incorporate into our lives. Human beings need commandments. We need to marry our freedom (Pesach) to Torah (Shavuot), to *mitzvah*. We need both. In the summer of our lives, one of the most important tasks is to discover God's *mitzvah* for ourselves.

Take a look at the chaos in your own life, the places where you are out of control. How can *mitzvah* help to bring a sense of order back into your life?

Surely, this mitzvah which I command you this day is not so baffling for you, nor is it out of reach. It is not in the heavens that one could say, "Who will go up to heaven for us so that we can understand it and do it?" Neither is it beyond the sea that one could say, "Who will cross the sea and bring it to us so that we can understand it and do it?" Rather, it is very close to you. It is in your mouths and in your hearts, waiting to be fulfilled.

— DEUTERONOMY 30:11–14

How do we start? How do we begin? The whole thing about doing commandments seems so far away from where we are, from how we have lived our lives. And what if I do start? Will my whole life change? Will I become one of those awful religious fanatics who seem to have a pat answer for everything?

The questions are not new; only the circumstances from which we ask them are. And the answer hasn't changed much either. You do not have to look very far. You need not travel to exotic places. You don't even have to ask anyone else. It's right there. On the tip of your tongue. In your heart. Nowhere else. Waiting to be fulfilled.

What is the *mitzvah* in your heart? Look inside. What is the *mitzvah* in your mouth? Speak the words.

> *Rabbi Huna and Rabbi Jeremiah said in the name of Rabbi Hiyya bar Abba: It is written, "They have forsaken Me and have not kept My Torah" (Jeremiah 16:11). This is to say, "If only they had forsaken Me, but kept My Torah! Since they then would have been occupied with it, the light which is in it would have restored them to the right path."*
>
> — LAMENTATIONS RABBAH

People ask me all the time, "Rabbi, how do I find God? How do I get a sense of God's presence into my life?" They see that as a first step. As the place to begin. And for some, it can be that way. But Judaism suggests another approach as equally viable. Do a *mitzvah*. Forget about God and just do a *mitzvah*. Because inherent in that action will be a spark of light, released by the very doing, that, together with other sparks, will illuminate a path to God.

What is the *mitzvah* you have been waiting to do? Let today be the day.

> *The prohibition against making idols includes the prohibition of making idols out of mitzvot. We should never imagine that the whole purpose of the mitzvah is its outer form (the doing); rather,*

---

it is its inward meaning (the devotion with which it was intended).

— Rabbi Menachem Mendl of Kotzk

We are so worried about doing it right. And because so many of us feel incompetent in Judaism, we avoid the embarrassment and distance ourselves from doing the very things that would heal us and make us whole. Then there are others who become religious behaviorists, filling their lives with more and more doing just for doing's sake. They use their doing as a weapon, as a badge of honor, as a wedge between themselves and those they deem as "nonobservant."

But there is a path through this Scylla and Charybdis. And it lies in the intention we bring to our doing. Nobody is keeping score. We don't rack up *mitzvot* like some sort of trophy. We do them one at a time, trying to bring the totality of our being to each and every *mitzvah*. That is all God asks of us. That is all God expects. And it is enough.

Think of a *mitzvah* you would like to do today. It could be anything from helping the homeless to lighting a candle. Choose one. Then do it with all your heart and do not tell anyone (at least for today) what you have done.

One mitzvah leads to another, just as one sin leads to another.

— Pirke Avot 4:2

I like to think of *mitzvah* as taking a step closer to God, and sin as taking a step away. All of our lives are a dance—now forward, now backward, two steps forward, three back . . . and on it goes. That is just the way it is, a component of our being human. But there comes a point in our dance when we realize that we are, in fact, in spite of all our backsliding, getting closer. At that moment, each *mitzvah* will lead us to the next one. I am not sure how that happens, but I have seen it enough times to know that it does. The important thing is to begin.

Remember those game boards that have a path printed on them (like Candy Land)? Imagine your life as that path. Think of the last *mitzvah* you have done as one box on the path. See yourself doing that *mitzvah*. Now look to the next empty box. Keep focusing on it until the next *mitzvah* appears. Repeat.

~~ ~~ ~~

meditations

TIKKUN OLAM/
REPAIRING THE WORLD

In the process of God's self-disclosure or emanation, sparks of divine light accidentally and disastrously became embedded in all material things. These sparks of light yearn to be liberated from their imprisoned state and return to their source within the Godhead, thus restoring the original divine unity.

— LAWRENCE FINE, *SAFED SPIRITUALITY*

Our world is a world of broken vessels, with sparks of Divine light everywhere. Our task is to repair the world and heal its inhabitants, releasing the sparks through conscious action. We are fixers, cosmic repairmen and -women, attempting to restore the unity that has been shattered. This was not God's original plan, but it is the way things turned out. Just look around. We know the world in which we live is far from perfection. Perhaps the world was just not ready for the pure light. Perhaps we could not handle it. Perhaps it is in the very nature of the physical realm to be imperfect and incomplete. Whatever the reason, the world is still waiting to be redeemed. And we have work to do.

Can you see the sparks? They are everywhere. Try to imagine them in everyone and in everything as you go through your day. Where will it be (most) difficult to see them? In whom? What can you do to release them?

Salvation is attained, not by subscription to metaphysical dogmas, but solely by love of God expressed in action.

— HASDAI CRESCAS

We spend so much of our lives looking for truth in complex ideas. We want to shape our lives around a philosophical principle, an ideology, a theology that puts all the pieces together for us. Yet Judaism insists that God is to be found in the common deed, in the so-called trivial moments of life. It is by doing that we attain ultimate truth. Simple actions. That's it.

What actions will you take today to heal and repair the world? Think about it. The possibilities are literally endless.

Rabbi Tarfon used to say: The day is short, the task is multiple, the workers are lazy, the reward is great, and the Master of the House is pressing.

— PIRKE AVOT 2:20

Doesn't sound as if we have much of a chance, does it? What with a short day, lots to do, unenthusiastic helpers, and an impatient Boss, how will we ever complete the task—a world healed of its brokenness and pain? Yet, one thing draws us on. We have been promised a great reward. And what could be greater than *tikkun olam*? A world healed and perfected.

In every generation there have been those who have been driven by this vision. They are the peacemakers, the ones who feed the hungry and shelter the homeless, who practice random acts of kindness, who treat others as they themselves would like to be treated, who respect and care for our planet and its creatures. There has always been much to do. There still is.

Have you been lazy? Overwhelmed by the task? God does not ask us as individuals to complete the task, just to do our share. How will you repair the world, today?

We may say of this generation that it possesses knowledge; but everybody desires only his own perfection and is not concerned with the community. Salvation, however, hinges upon one's desire for the perfection of the world.
— EIGHTEENTH-CENTURY HASIDIC TEXT

We think that "me-ism" came to us in the 1980s, that ours was the first generation in the history of the world to deal with the problem of self-centeredness. But the notion that I can save myself and not have to worry about anyone else is as old as we are; it merely takes on different forms at different times. And it is always an illusion.

The truth is, we are connected, you and I. We may appear as separate, and, of course, to some extent we are. I have my own name, and family . . . I do my work in the world . . . I have a personal history. But I am also linked to you, to all that was, and to all that will ever be. The cells in my body, the air I breathe—these at one time may have been yours, or someone else's. Our destinies are intertwined.

Have you focused on your own perfection to the neglect of the community? Did you think you could accomplish this alone? How will you express your concern for the community, today? Tomorrow?

The basic principle is, of course, not purity for its own sake, but the need to bring all things in the world to the state of tikkun or perfection, to raise them up by correcting, remedying, and setting them right, to re-create a thing by stripping it to its essential, to redeem it by allowing it to be its utmost.

— RABBI ADIN STEINSALTZ

Tikkun olam is not an abstraction. It is not a theory meant to be discussed in classrooms. It is a course of action, a plan, a way of directing our attention and behavior. There is in each of us and in every thing an essential core, our raison d'être, the very reason we were put here on earth. Somehow that gets all covered up, masked, disguised. We lose our way. We forget where we were going, or even that we were going. Through *tikkun* we strip away all the junk, allowing each of us to be the person we were meant to be, allowing everyone and every thing to fulfill his/her/its particular task.

Focus on your central core, that which makes you you. Visualize all the things (behavior, attitudes, actions, etc.) that interfere with your becoming or block you from being your utmost. Now imagine each one of those things being peeled off of you. That is *tikkun*. That is what the world (and everything in it) requires.

Therefore our hope is in You, Adonai our God, soon to behold the glory of your strength, to remove false gods from the earth, to abolish idolatry, to repair and perfect the world under the rule of Shaddai.

— DAILY PRAYERBOOK

Repair of the world is our task, but it is also God's. We cannot do this work alone or accomplish it all by ourselves. God has to help. Our hope is in Adonai. First, all of our idolatries, all of the things with which we have supplanted God in our hearts, must be removed, must be no more. Idols are not simply statues; they are the individuals, the things, ideas, and beliefs to which we give power over our lives. Only when this work is done can we hope to see a world in which everyone will come to know the One True God of the Universe—one God which makes us one human family on earth. This has been our Jewish hope for the last two thousand years. It is our hope, still.

What "idols" are keeping you from God? Ask for God's help in removing them from your life.

᠁   ᠁   ᠁

meditations

COMMUNITY

Do not separate yourself from the community.
— PIRKE AVOT 2:4

One of our "sacred" American images is that of the lone cowboy riding off on his horse into the sunset. He is our hero—free, independent, self-sufficient, the one who does not need anyone else to make his world complete. This is the exact opposite of the Jewish ideal.

There are more words in the Hebrew language for "community" than there are for any other term as with Eskimos and their many words for "snow." Hillel urges us to stay connected to the community because Judaism is, more than anything else, a communal enterprise. We have long believed that our salvation as well as our demise is linked to our people as a whole. We rise and fall as a group. Yet it is sometimes difficult to want to be a part of this community. We see qualities that we just do not admire or even like. We do not want to be associated with some of the excesses, or with those people we deem as (unlike ourselves) "not spiritual." Much of the community seems centered on issues that are not our own. Sometimes it is embarrassing; other times it feels like dead weight, the proverbial albatross around one's neck.

When do you feel yourself wanting to separate from the community? What steps have you already taken to distance yourself? What steps can you take to (begin to) return?

The autonomous Jewish self derives its autonomy as part of the people of Israel's covenant partnership with God. Such a Judaism knows no isolated, atomistic, worthy self. Rather, selfhood itself necessarily involves God, people, and history.

— RABBI EUGENE BOROWITZ

We only appear to be autonomous. The truth is, what we call selfhood derives from our connection to others—to our parents, our people, our God. We become a Jew by being entered into the covenant. The covenant is a communal agreement, begun with Abraham and Sarah, but binding on all their descendants, including everyone who has ever chosen the path of Judaism for him/herself. We are all the children of the first patriarch and matriarch.

There is no such thing as an individual Jew. Our attempts to "do Judaism" to the exclusion of the community will ultimately meet with frustration and failure. Even this workout is not enough, which is why I provide only six meditations for each theme week. While the reality of our lives makes it difficult (if not impossible) to be part of a daily minyan/community, we need to remind ourselves at least once a week, ideally Shabbat, of who and what we really are, by plugging into our people.

Imagine yourself as a link in a chain that stretches back into time and off into the future. Keep the image for as long as you can.

Of the four species used in Sukkot, the etrog has both taste and fragrance, the myrtle has fragrance but no taste, the lulav bears fruit which has taste but no fragrance, and the willow has neither taste nor fragrance. All four species must be taken together. The absence of any one makes the mitzvah incomplete.

— MIDRASH

A community is made up of many different types of people. Each one brings a particular set of talents and abilities; each one has a role to play. And each one, sooner or later, will have his/her day—including the person we deem as useless or unnecessary. We cannot afford to write off anyone. Everyone is part of the whole, and is needed.

We live in a time in which there is great diversity in the Jewish community. The struggle over defining who is a Jew and who will determine Jewish status is played out in newspapers, in political back rooms, and in the *Knesset* in Israel. In our own synagogues and *havurot*/organizations and institutions, there is always that one person who drives us a little crazy, who does not seem to pull his/her own weight, that one person we wish was just not there. You know who I mean.

Whom have you written off? Whom have you placed outside the community? Envision that person as part of the whole. See the community as incomplete, missing something without him/her.

When the two Hebrew letter "yuds" stand alongside each other, then it represents God. If one "yud" is above the other, then this is not God. This shows that things have come to an end. And so it is. When we stand alongside each other, God is with us. If we consider ourselves above another, we have reached the end.

— HASIDIC TEACHING

We are bound, one to the other. And the very presence of God as a living reality is also bound up with our ability to get along, to see the other as essential, to see the other as my equal, my partner. How can I expect to have God in my life, when I cannot even get along with another human being? Though the path is often lonely, I cannot do this work alone. And I cannot even entertain the idea of my wholeness while I place myself above the other, any other.

Think about it. Look around. Whom do you think of as "below" you? Imagine yourselves as two Hebrew letter "yuds." Try to bring them into balance, each one standing alongside the other.

Pray for all, be kind to all, and do for all, but do not forget who you are. Keep together, and your togetherness will keep you.
— SAGES

Every one of us lives with this tension—universal versus particular. How can I be a part of the world around me and at the same time maintain my Jewish identity? We think of it as a new problem, but, in truth, it is as old as our people. The Torah itself warns us to distance ourselves from the "gods" of the surrounding nations.

In their battle with this issue, some have been swallowed up entirely. They assimilate in thought and deed, becoming indistinguishable from their non-Jewish neighbors. Others feel they must go in the opposite extreme, living in self-contained neighborhoods, dressing in clothes that isolate them from the mainstream, surrounding themselves at work and at home with Jews and Jews alone. Most of us want to be somewhere in the middle. And we can. We can love our neighbors and be part of the world, and at the same time remember who we are.

Where are you in this struggle? Do you feel comfortable with the mix? Or do you need to balance it one way or the other?

And the priest shall go forth out of the camp . . .
— LEVITICUS 14:3

Exclusion from the community was seen, and is seen to this day, as the harshest punishment in the world, in some ways even worse than death. Yet we see here that the hand that excludes is the same hand that must include. The one who sent the *metzora*/leper away must be the one who goes out and performs the ritual of purification, enabling the now healed individual to come back into the camp.

We are quick to exclude others. And sometimes, this exclusion wounds them so deeply that it is difficult for them to ever return. That is why it is our job to find them, begin the process of healing, and bring them back. Every soul is precious. When we diminish our community by even one, we are all diminished.

Whom have you excluded from your life? What can you do to bring them back?

FAST OF (17TH) TAMMUZ—TISHA (9TH) B'AV—THREE WEEKS OF REBUKE

~

For the Jewish calendar, most of the summer and the beginning of fall is seen as a time of preparation or getting ready for the High Holy Days. Beginning with the 17th of Tammuz (traditionally, a day of fasting), we enter a ten-week period of repairing and strengthening our relationship with God. The first three weeks which end with another Fast Day—Tisha b'Av—are called the "*shlosha d'tochacha*/three of rebuke" and the last seven are called the "*shevah d'nehemtah*/seven of consolation." For three weeks we focus on our sins, and then for seven we hear that, in spite of them, God wants us back. (In the synagogue, we hear this message through the weekly prophetic reading known as the "haftarah.") If we do this work properly, the High Holy Days become a time in which we can declare God "*Avinu*/our Father-parent" and "*Malkeinu*/our King-Ruler," and really mean it. It can also become a time of self-acceptance and acceptance of limits.

meditations

SELF-REPROACH—TAKING A HARD LOOK AT OURSELVES

Only as a soul comes to know itself can it come to know its Creator.

— IBN EZRA

The promise of the High Holy Days is that we can right our relationship with God. No matter how far we have strayed, no matter how many sins we may have committed moving us away from the Holy One, God welcomes us back with open arms. And it begins with a process of coming clean with ourselves, of introspection and honest self-evaluation, of owning our shortcomings and stopping our excuses for them. Knowing God, having a relationship with the One does not mean we take on a list of behaviors defined by others and start doing them. Rather, it begins with really and truly getting to know ourselves. It is that simple and that difficult. A true spiritual path requires self-awareness. The behaviors will come later. And they, too, will have to resonate with our inner selves. What works for one human being will not necessarily work for another. We cannot lose ourselves if we want to find God.

What are the things you want to know about yourself? Write down the questions you would like to ask yourself this year. Then spend some portion of your daily meditation asking the questions, one question at a time, or one question each day. Don't try to answer them. Just ask. The answers will come. (Sometimes it is difficult to do this work all by yourself; rabbis, good friends, psychotherapists, and others all can be helpers in the process of getting to know yourself.)

See, this alone I have discovered. God made humans straight, but they have sought a multitude of calculations.

— ECCLESIASTES 7:29

We do not start out that way, but somehow our lives get very complicated. As children, we were innocent and free of guile. We spoke our minds without weighing the consequences. We played games, freely imagined worlds of others, happily spent our days. And then, it began to shift. Our concern became what others thought of us, how we fit in, what would be appropriate, what we could get away with in any given situation. We did not plan it that way—it just happened. And we continue because we assume that this is just the way of the world. Besides, we say, everyone acts this way.

But we cannot hide from ourselves forever. Sooner or later we need to take a look at all the calculations and distortions that keep us from being ourselves and keep us from being at one with God. Picture yourself as standing straight. That is who you are. Now consider all the things that cause you to bend or slouch. As you rid yourself of each of these, imagine yourself getting straighter and straighter.

That you come before Me with your offerings and your prayers, who asked that of you? I cannot bear iniquity with solemn gatherings.

— ISAIAH 1:12–13

A previous generation of Jews read these words as a proof text for giving up on ritual actions. But that was a misreading. Isaiah does not tell us to stop observing Shabbat, stop coming to Temple, stop offering sacrifices. Rather, he says that if we do these things while not living a life of righteousness and justice (especially when it comes to dealing with the powerless in society) then our actions are most hateful to God. It is hypocrisy that Isaiah decries. If we thought we could appear "religious on the outside" while thinking, feeling, doing whatever we wanted to on the inside, then the prophet comes along to tell us that this is what God cannot abide. God calls us to both—ritual acts and ethical conduct. Both together, not either/or.

Take a look at your life and the balance that is either there or not there (yet). Where do you need to place the emphasis? Are you coming before God trying to get away without one or the other?

Any kind of injustice, corruption, cruelty desecrates the very essence of the prayer adventure, since it encases us in an ugly little world into which God is unwilling to enter. If we crave to meet God . . . then we must purge ourselves of all that separates us from God.

— JOSEPH B. SOLOVEITCHIK

One of the things that I hear so often is that even for those who honestly seek the One, God is so very difficult to find. It is as if we are looking for a clear and definitive sign of God's existence—a miracle, a parting sea, a resounding voice that everyone can hear. But would that really do it? Didn't our ancient ancestors in the wilderness get all those things and still have crises in faith? After all, they were the ones who built the golden calf, declaring, "This is our God!"

The Torah teaches us that signs and wonders do not automatically create and sustain belief. Actually, it is the other way around. It has to do with our personal receptivity; otherwise, miracles can be doubted or forgotten. Evidence of God is all around us. We need to work on that which keeps God out.

What is it that separates you from God, and from realizing Adonai's presence in your life? This is the time for purging all those elements that separate you from the One. What are they? Make a list. Ask God's help in shedding them, one at a time.

One is not free from conditions. But one is free to take a stand in regard to them.

— VIKTOR FRANKL

The world is not an illusion. The pain brought to us by others and by the world itself is real. There are things we simply cannot change. And there are circumstances that are truly beyond our control. This is reality. But we can always choose our response. And we can change ourselves. How we respond to a situation, any situation, is always our choice.

And thus we see two people go through a similar experience; one is destroyed by it, his life embittered, while the other is deepened by it, her life made sweeter. We all have conditions that frame our lives, but it is our response to those conditions that makes us fully human.

What conditions are you blaming for the unhappiness, misfortune, and negativity that exist in your life? How can you (begin to) change your stance in regard to them?

In my youth, I thought I would convert the whole world to God. But soon I discovered that it would be enough to convert the people in my town. Then I realized that my program was still too ambitious, and I concentrated on the persons in my household. Finally, it dawned on me—I must work upon myself, so that I may give true service to God.

— CHAIM HALBERSTAM

How much time and effort we spend trying to fix everyone! This is our immaturity deceiving us that it is "them" and not ourselves who need the work. But the only God relationship we can set right is our own. And the only way to do that is to work on ourselves. Leave God's part to God; you will not be disappointed.

What work is left for you to do? Where is the leftover resistance? What are you holding on to? Which steps are you still afraid to take? Where are you faking it? Work on yourself. Be yourself. It is only you that God wants.

❧   ❧   ❧

meditations
FAILURE

God before whom words must be true, we acknowledge our faults and our failings.

— SELICHOT PRAYER

How simple and yet how difficult to say these words. We are not perfect. We have faults and we fail. So why is it that we do not want to admit it? What is it about ourselves that we are protecting, defending, holding on to?

I grew up being told that I could be anything I wanted to be, if only I would apply myself to the task. My parents were probably trying to build my self-esteem, but in the long run, it had the opposite effect. Nothing I did was ever good enough, because I was supposedly capable of better. And anytime I fell short of the mark, it had to have been because I did not try hard enough. And so I refused to fail, and hid it (from myself and others) when I inevitably did. Part of the beginning of our return to self and God is the admission of our faults and failings. God does not need this admission; the Lord knows. It is we who must say the words.

Acknowledge your faults and your failings. You may want to write a list. Speak them out loud.

You don't stumble because you are weak; you stumble because you think you are strong.

— YIDDISH FOLK SAYING

Oh, the games we play with ourselves. Pretending we are what we are not and sometimes even fooling ourselves. If only we could admit that we are weak and needy and be okay with that. It would save us lots of bumps and bruises when we stumble and fall.

We all have real strengths. No one asks that we deny those. This is not about false modesty. But it is about trying to understand how and why we fail, and what we might do to break the cycle of such failure. We think we are strong. Look again. We are not. Nor do we have to be. We have strengths, real strengths, but we are not strong. And it is our pretending that we are that keeps us sprawled out on the ground.

What are your weaknesses? Write them down. They belong to you, are part of yourself, part of what makes you you. They're nothing to be ashamed of. Nothing to hide. If you can, share them with a trusted friend.

It is a command to cast the lots but if he failed to do so, [the service] is, nevertheless, valid.

— TALMUD, YOMA 39B

We tend to believe that so much is riding on what we do and how we do it. We often think that if we do not get all the details just right, then everything will fall apart. So much of our self-help literature (I confess, I read it while in the bookstore,) places us in the driver's seat that is our life. When reading that stuff, I get the feeling that if I just got it all right, then my life would be perfect—it is totally up to me. But my experience has taught me that the fabric that is life can be missing a thread every now and then and still hold together, still be beautiful, still provide comfort and warmth.

Think about your failures, large and small. How did they affect the outcome of what you were working on? What turned out fine, in spite of the fact that you failed to do something?

The temptation to do evil (which exists in each of us) gets stronger every day.

— TALMUD, SUKKOT 52A

We have this naive notion that once we really get our act together, we will be beyond all the pitfalls and strivings of our earlier days of struggle. While experience can bring us insight, it will never remove us from the reality of having to live our lives. And those lives will have all of the same elements they have always had. In fact, as the Talmud indicates, it might even get a bit tougher. The greater we are, the greater our opportunity for failure. It is not just that there is less room at the top, though that is certainly true. Rather, it actually gets more subtle, more nuanced once we get the broad strokes down. We see things in our world and in ourselves that might have escaped us earlier. We begin to hold ourselves accountable at a much higher level. And all the while, the force for evil within us, that force which would deter us, detain us, knock us off our path, grows at the same intensity. It is a prescription for failure. No wonder we say, "How the mighty have fallen!"

Take a good look at the *Yetzer haRa*/evil inclination within yourself. Feel how its force has grown as you have grown. Where is it leading you now? What will you do to resist and overcome its power?

Moses did not enter the Promised Land, not because his life was too short, but because it was a human life.

— MARTIN BUBER

Some of our failures will occur because we will simply run out of time. There is no way we can accomplish, or be, or say, or see all the things we want to in one lifetime. No matter how successful we are, there will always be something left undone. As human beings we are subject to the clock, and it is always running.

But there will be other failures as well. Real failures. And these we will not be able to blame on the clock or on others. They will be our failures and we will have to learn to accept them even as we accept ourselves. These are the failures that occur because we are human. Every person fails. Every person. Even you and me. We are not failures; but we fail, nevertheless.

What are the failures you are carrying around in your heart? Say out loud, "I have failed at _____." You can also make a list: "My Failures for This Year."

This is why Scripture reproved Jehoshua, for in all other passages it is spelled "Jehoshua," but here it is spelled "Joshua." Why did Joshua, who had the power of the Holy Land to assist him, fail to pray for mercy?

— TALMUD, ARACHIN 32B

It does not seem like such a big failure. Joshua thought that the holiness of the land itself would heal the people of their idolatrous desires and practices. He did not think it required any intervention on his part. But he was wrong, and was held accountable. The diminution of his name is seen as a diminution of the man himself.

The harsh truth is that some of our failures do change us and our reality. From some failures there is no or only partial recovery. We may not like to hear that, but it is true. We cannot always return to (exactly) the way things were. Some failures are unalterable. For these, we can only ask forgiveness, and try to move on with our lives. Do you have some failures like these, that have changed you forever? Have you forgiven yourself yet? Have you asked for forgiveness? What are you waiting for? Perhaps this can be the year when you finally accept what you have done and move on.

~~ ~~ ~~

m e d i t a t i o n s
SIN

*For there is no one on earth so righteous as to do good without
sinning.*

— ECCLESIASTES 7:20

For many Jews, the word "sin" sounds very Christian, and has
very heavy overtones. Actually, the Hebrew words *chatat, avone,*
and *peshah,* though usually translated as "sin," mean "missed the
mark," "turned away," and "strayed from the path," respectively.
The Jewish sense is that we are all on our way to do the right thing,
but somehow we don't always get there. *T'shuvah,* usually translated as "repentance" (which again sounds very Christian to us),
really means "return," or "getting back on track." It's not very
heavy at all.

I understand sin as those actions or words that take us away
from God (and *mitzvah* as that which brings us closer). Every
mitzvah is a step toward God; every sin a step away. And all our
lives are a dance—two steps forward, one step back, three steps
back, four steps forward. These first weeks of our preparation for
the High Holy Days invite us to look at all our backward steps.

I suggest you write them down, but warn you that this can be a
very painful process. Keep the list and bring it with you on Yom
Kippur. You can read it during one of the confessional prayers.
Imagine God as a parent with arms outstretched waiting for your
embrace. For each item on your list, imagine yourself taking a step
away.

On the first day of Sukkot we begin reckoning our sins.
— MIDRASH

Sukkot, which is called *'z'man simcha'teinu*/the season of our joy, falls only five days after Yom Kippur. After that full day of fasting and self-reflection, of honestly examining our lives and resolving to do better, of feeling good about our return to the path of God, just five days later we start looking at our sins again. Our tradition recognizes and accepts the fact that sinning is part of the human condition. If we begin reckoning our sins right away after Yom Kippur, perhaps they will not seem so overwhelming. Perhaps they will not get away from us or go undetected. And if we look at them during the festival most associated with joy, perhaps we will lighten the burden we feel at having taken some more steps away from our covenantal partner, God.

Okay. Take out the list you made yesterday. Look at each item once again. Look at them with a feeling of joy in your heart. Let that feeling help you in your resolve to do better, to move closer to the One who patiently waits for us all.

For I acknowledge my iniquity, and my sin is ever before me.
— PSALM 51:5

It begins this way. We must own our sins. All the rationalizations, all passing of responsibility to someone else, all the excuses must be put aside in order for us to do this work. I am a sinner. I cannot hide from my sins. I must look at them and confront them even as they confront me. This is not a comfortable moment, nor is it meant to be. My skin is flush. It is hard to sit still. My eyes want to look down, I want to avert my gaze, to not be seen by others or by God. But there is nowhere to hide now. It is time to acknowledge our guilt, to own it, and to confess.

Say it out loud. "I acknowledge my iniquity. My sin is ever

before me." Say it again. And again. This honesty, painful as it might be, is the beginning of our healing, the beginning of our getting straight with ourselves, with others, and with God. It is a step we have to take, each and every year, each and every day.

All sins are attempts to fill voids.

— SIMONE WEIL

None of us are complete, at least not all of the time. There are tasks undone, business unfinished, goals to be achieved, accomplishments awaiting our time and energy. On top of all that, many of us sense that no matter what we do, somehow it is not enough. We are never enough. Sin, taking steps away from God, is one way we attempt to fill this void. But the trouble is, sin can never do it. Sin, though bringing us temporary pleasure or power (after all, that is why we engage in it), will always be transitory, leaving us even more empty, wanting more. Sin can never fill us up.

What voids exist in your life? What sins have you committed/are you committing in order to feel full and complete?

The one who has not tasted sin is not qualified for the holy.

— *Author unknown*

We often think of "holy" as perfect or without blemish. Actually, in Hebrew "holy" (*kadosh*) means "separate" or "sanctified to God." If sins are those actions that take us away from the Holy One, then our quote tells us that unless we have felt this distance, unless we know what it feels like to live without God, we will never be able to grasp the holy. Sin, then, becomes a necessary step in the life of holiness. We will never have one without the other.

Another way of looking at this is to understand that even within the sin there is a spark of holiness, and vice versa—every moment of holiness is tinged with a drop of sin. Every quality contains its opposite. In fact, it may be a necessary ingredient. The Taoists called this "yin/yang" and the psychologist Carl Jung described it as "the shadow." In Jewish mystical terminology it is the *sitra d'atra*. We do not know how it works. But it seems to be the reality of the universe. Everything contains its opposite.

Which sins that you have tasted have qualified you for the holy, have made you better able to sense the holy in your life?

> *"Come now and let us reason together," says Adonai, "If your sins be like crimson, they can turn white as snow; if they are red as dyed wool, they can become like fleece."*
>
> — ISAIAH 1:18

We all sin, there is no escaping the fact. But we are not condemned by these sins. Nor are our lives permanently and negatively transformed by them. We sometimes feel that what we have done is so bad, so terrible, that we can never return to a sense of purity or wholeness. The prophet reminds us that this is not the case.

Imagine if we had to carry all our sins for a lifetime. Who could bear up under such a burden? But Judaism is a most humanistic system. It allows us to cast off our sins, to transform them, no matter how "stained" we may have become by them. If they can change from red to white, there is hope for all of us.

Think of those things you have done that you would consider "red." Through your letting go of them, watch them (in your mind's eye) lose their color and turn white.

SEVEN WEEKS
OF CONSOLATION

meditations
T'SHUVAH/RETURN

When God finished the six days of creating, there followed a holy period of possibility when the miraculous was sewn into the fabric of creation, to unfold when it was appropriate, when it was needed. Dusk, when the sixth day had ended, the night not yet begun, that time of mystery and uncertainty, when something had ended, something new not yet begun, that time called "between the suns," this is when t'shuvah was created.

— JAMES STONE GOODMAN (ADAPTED FROM THE TALMUD)

So *t'shuvah* (literally, "return") is part of the cosmic plan of creation. It is as if God understood that we human beings, perhaps because we are human, would retreat or withdraw from this relationship with the Holy One of Being. Sometimes that withdrawal is conscious or willful; we deny or reject God, our role as Jews, the commandments which seek to sanctify our lives. But much of the time, we simply don't think about it, or we fill our lives with other things that also seem important. Most of us are not evil. We simply lack knowledge and awareness, we are lazy, we make poor choices, we are imperfect. In the end, we back-burner our relationship with God, unconsciously placing it somewhere lower on the agenda. Or not on the agenda at all.

But the miracle is, God never gives up on us. Return is always possible. We are not condemned to the past. Anything is possible. What is something new that you would like to begin this year? It could be a project, a relationship, a way of behaving or thinking. You can break an old habit, let go of something you have been holding on to, stop self-destructing. This is the time. "Between the suns." One year is ending and a brand-new one about to begin. Don't wait for a crisis. You can take the first step today.

To atone is to be at one with God, to sink self into the not-self, to achieve a mystic unity with the Source of Being.

— ISAAC GOLDBERG

I believe we all long for oneness. All of creation does. In some sense we are already there, for where can we be that God is not? Yet, much of the time we sense ourselves as separate. And, of course, this is painful. Many of us have sought the oneness through relationships, through sex, through alcohol and drugs. While these have brought us the feeling of merger, they are only temporary. Sooner or later we wake up and realize that we still feel alone and adrift. The pain is still there.

To make *t'shuvah* means to return to the Source of All Being. Return means we have already been there. We know the way. It will mean a letting go. It will require our getting out of the way of ourselves. It is the only at-oneness that has lasting effect in our lives.

Lie flat on a bed or the floor. Sink down into a comforter. Imagine there is no separation between you and that upon which you are lying. Let that become the physical or symbolic action for the spiritual work you will need to do.

Longing, I sought Your presence
Lord, with my whole heart did I call and pray

And going out toward You,
I found You coming to me on the way.
RABBI JUDAH HALEVI

The poet suggests a process, a methodology for finding God in our lives. It is the path of the heart, of prayer. If we want to find God, we must seek the One with longing, with all our hearts. If we make such a move toward the Holy One, then we will find God coming toward us. But it begins with us. We must make the first move. It is what the Torah tells us happened at Mount Sinai as well. Moses went up the mountain and God came down, meeting him halfway. Many of us would like for God to just be there for us, on demand. And sometimes, we are graced in just that way. But for most of us, having a sense of God takes work, effort, movement on our parts. Can you take a step toward God in your life? What are you afraid of? What are you waiting for?

All that the Creator demands is that a person make a beginning
in the right direction; thereafter, God will aid him/her to continue
on the right path.

— RABBI NOAH LEKHIVITZER

Again, we hear, it is up to us to begin. We do not have to get there all the way on our own efforts. God is our true partner in this work. God will help us, will bring us along. But we have to start the journey. Many of us are waiting for a sign. Even more are skeptical. Some have rejected the reality of God altogether. These are the times in which we live, in which we have always lived. Do you think the ones who created a golden calf and said "*This* is our God!" were any better? Doubt is not a modern invention. It is part of the human condition. Perhaps that is why it has to begin with us. We must take a step, a few steps against the void that is our doubt. We must take a risk, show that we are worthy, that we are willing to put something of ourselves into the process, to stand out against the crowd. And then God will be our helper. Take a step. Then, ask God to help you the rest of the way.

If one does t'shuvah and then reverts to the sin, it is no t'shuvah.

— PESIQTA RABBATI

We have all been asked this question: "What good is making *t'shuvah,* saying you are sorry, if all you are going to do is go out and do the same old thing again and again?" And the answer is twofold. If we are sincerely sorry at the time of our *t'shuvah,* if our intention is pure and our motivation true, then our return is for the good. Remember, *t'shuvah* is a humanistic attempt on the part of Judaism to allow us to go on with our lives without having to carry the heavy baggage of every sin, every error, every mistake we have ever made.

But on another level, our *t'shuvah* is never fully complete unless when given an opportunity to commit the same sin, we refrain from doing so. And that is a challenge we face every day. That is why the alcoholic must say, "I am an alcoholic," never "I was an alcoholic," no matter how long s/he has been on the wagon. One can always revert to a previous sin. And often we do. Such is the dance of life.

What sins do you think you are done with? Which negative patterns keep reappearing in your life? Accept these as your life issues. Say to yourself, "I am a _____ ." Ask God's help in making a complete *t'shuvah* this year.

Repentance should be realized through joy.

— REBBE NACHMAN OF BRATZLAV

Okay. This repentance stuff is heavy work. You have been thinking about your sins every day, feeling sorry, crying a little, maybe even feeling a bit depressed about how far you have strayed from God and God's will for you. So Rebbe Nachman comes along to remind us to put the joy back into the work. It is like a diet: You can get depressed over all the weight you need to lose, or you can feel good about all the pounds you have already taken off. Remember, becoming one with God is a dance. Not every step will be forward. It is all part of the dance. As you take each step, feel the joy of dancing.

Think of all the positive steps you have already taken since these ten weeks began. Write them down. Celebrate. Think of all the backsliding as well. The fact that you recognize them as such, that your consciousness has been raised in this regard, is also cause to celebrate.

~ ~ ~

m e d i t a t i o n s

L O V E

We all need to love. And we all need to be loved. Love makes us appreciate life more, enjoy it more, value it more. We are not alone; love makes us feel we belong to each other.
— DOROTHY K. KRUPKE

The world can be a very harsh and lonely place sometimes. It is love, more than anything else, that helps us break down the prison of isolation we feel. Both the love we give and the love we receive. For what is love but a willingness to extend beyond ourselves, to take risks, to be there for another, and to trust that the other will be there for us.

The loving relationship is so ecstatic because it is the human epitome of the yearning for oneness that pervades the entire cosmos. That is what we mean when we say the prayer known as the *Sh'ma*. We say that God is One. Everything in the world hungers for unity. God is the ultimate unity. The ultimate oneness. When we love without ulterior motives, when we love wholeheartedly, when the boundaries of self disappear, for that moment we achieve a oneness with the other, the world, with everything around us. We overcome our loneliness through conscious acts of loving. God dwells in the presence of such love.

Think of all the people you really and truly love and by whom you need to be loved. Let them know. Today.

> *Falling in love is a temporary escape from the loneliness of our individual ego boundaries to a feeling of merger with our beloved, and with all of life.*
>
> — M. SCOTT PECK

The sudden release from the isolation of self is experienced by most of us as ecstatic. We and our beloved are one. All things are possible. The strength of our love will enable us to overcome any obstacle. We are lonely no more. But sooner or later, in response to the reality of living, individual identity will reassert itself. She wants to go to Temple; he wants to watch the game on television. She wants to save money; he "needs" that Jaguar. She does not like his friends; to tell you the truth, he does not like hers either. Once again, they are two separate individuals. They have "fallen out of love," or so they think.

As products of modernity, we keep looking for romantic love to fulfill us, to make us complete. We have bought this package, and when we do not feel it, we think something is wrong, something is missing in our relationships. Romantic love, while exciting and seemingly all-encompassing, is, in fact, transitory. It can never sustain itself. The honeymoon always ends. Ultimately, it becomes a kind of narcissism, a deadening of self to the world. And it cannot be the only way to understand love. Have you ever "fallen in love"? Are you "in love" now? Can you appreciate the feeling without equating it with love itself?

To love somebody is not just a strong feeling—it is a decision, it is a judgment, it is a promise.

— ERICH FROMM

We must understand that romantic love is merely the beginning of, not the basis for, a relationship. It creates a willingness to begin, to be there for one another, and to overlook (consciously or subconsciously) differences. When a couple comes to talk to me about their desire to marry, somewhere in that first conversation I invariably ask, "Why? Why do you want to get married? Don't you realize that more than half the marriages in America end in divorce?" And they most always answer, "Because we love each other. We are so much alike. We have so much in common." "Of course you do," I respond, "otherwise you would not be here in the first place. Now why do you want to get married?"

What I am hoping is that they will begin to see that love is more than just a feeling that blurs all differences. In fact, true love asks us to recognize those differences and see them as strengths, as something we enjoy in the other, something that gives us balance, that makes us whole. Love thus becomes a decision, and not merely a feeling. A decision to accept the other as s/he really is, not as we imagined him/her to be.

Whom do you love? Is it a feeling or a decision, a judgment, a promise? All of the above?

Your love for Your people, the House of Israel, is unconditional and eternal . . .

— DAILY EVENING PRAYER

In this prayer, which we read right before the *Sh'ma Yisrael,* we say that God gave us commandments to guide our lives. A commandment enslaves and liberates us at the same time; it frees yet entraps us. On the one hand it gives us direction, so that we need not stumble blindly through life—that is freedom; on the other hand, it tells us how to spend our time and money, what to eat and not to eat, with whom we can associate, how to run our business, even how to speak appropriately to others, and those are limitations. Now, this act of giving commandments we call *ahavat olam*/eternal love. God loves us, so God limits our freedom, and God's freedom is limited as well. From now on, God is stuck with us and we are bound to the Holy One. We can have no other gods; God cannot choose another people as representatives. And this can be our paradigm for loving one another.

True love—and it matters not whether it is the love of spouse, or child, or country—involves a loss of freedom, a loss of autonomy, and to some extent, a loss of self. *Ahavat olam,* deep and abiding love, is having stake in the growth and well-being of others, in seeing them as whole in spite of their limitations and imperfections, in seeing them whole just the way they are.

Is your love for someone dependent on something? Whom do you love unconditionally? Can you love yourself in the same way?

Is that not the great childhood problem—and therefore the great human problem: to learn that it is good for you when other people love other people besides you? That I have a stake in their love? That I get more when others give to others.

— RABBI LAWRENCE KUSHNER

This reminds me of a song lyric from my childhood: "Love isn't something 'til you give it away." And yet, so many of us hold on to love as if it were a commodity, a finite substance that can get used up and spent. But unlike a commodity, love only grows the more we love. And the more the ones we love love others, the greater is their capacity, and the more love there will be in our world.

We hold on to love out of fear and insecurity, out of our sense of feeling unloved, out of the mistaken notion that all love must be sexual in order to be real, out of our lack of trust, out of the pain and wounds of having loved the wrong person. We insist that others love "only us" for the same reasons.

Where are you holding back in your love of others? Are you insisting (either verbally or internally) that someone love no one but you? Why?

We do not have to understand completely in order to love completely.
— NORMAN MACLEAN, *A RIVER RUNS THROUGH IT*

I believe this is so for every true love. Relationships call on us to accept without understanding; to contract ourselves, making room for the other; to be nurturing and be nurtured; to be needy and needed; to care at exactly the times we feel least able to; to join together physically and emotionally and yet to sense our separation as okay; to balance holding on with letting go; to make commitments and bind our lives by them; to be humble and admit our mistakes; to forgive and ask for forgiveness; to deny ourselves and delay gratification; to wait; to trust; to accept limits; to make sacrifices; to live by deeds and words and feelings; to be grateful and accepting of all that comes our way. This is love. And we need not understand any of it in order to live it, and be it.

Where in your life (and with whom) is there complete love? What, if anything, is holding you back in your other relationships?

᷒ ᷒ ᷒

meditations
RACHAMIM/COMPASSION

*Adonai, Adonai, God of compassion and grace, slow to anger,
abundant in loving kindness and truth.*

— EXODUS 34:6

In God's self-revelation to Moses, Adonai lists those attributes
by which we can come to know the Holy One. Moses wants to
"see" God. This is as close as he can get. Of those characteristics,
the first is compassion, *rachum* in Hebrew, *rachmunis* in Yiddish.
The Hebrew word for "womb" is *rechem,* and I believe these words
are related, for what is the womb but the ultimate place of
compassion, a place in which everything is given for the other?

God is compassion. God is a womb in which we receive
everything just because we are. And from this womb, we never have
to be born, never have to leave. As we begin our *t'shuvah*/return to
God, it is essential that we understand that it is we who have
separated ourselves from the Holy One. God desires our return.

If you are able, curl up in the fetal position. You are in God's
womb. Feel that. Know that everything you need is provided, and
will be provided. Say it: "God provides for me."

Have compassion for all, not only people but all living things.
— PATRIARCHS, ZEBULUN 5:1

It is rather easy to be compassionate toward the ones we love.
After all, they are a part of our lives and we are a part of theirs.

Though there are times when we argue, get angry, even hate, where there is love, there is bound to be compassion as well. But as God is compassionate to all of life, so are we challenged to be compassionate to everyone, to everything.

There is a midrash that tells of the moment in which the Egyptians and their chariots are drowning in the Sea of Reeds. The children of Israel have safely made it to the other side and are singing in praise of God. The angels rush into God's throne room and see the Holy One weeping. "Why are you crying?" they challenge. "Your children have escaped Pharaoh's trap!" "My children," God replies, "my children are drowning." That is compassion. This season challenges us to get in touch with our own compassion. Pretend that the world is your child, that everyone and everything in it are your children. How will that change the way you think of them? The way you act toward them?

A person must be very patient, even with himself.
— REBBE NACHMAN OF BRATZLAV

If it is good enough for everyone else, why not yourself? No one is any more (or less) worthy of God's compassion than you are. And if God can show you compassion, then can you do any less? We have become so self-critical, have set our standards so high, that we can often be quite cruel and destructive to ourselves. This is not the way it ought to be. We are God's children. We have to take care to show ourselves the same compassion as God does, to forgive ourselves, to allow room for mistakes and imperfections, for that is the way children grow to their wholeness and selfhood.

Say to yourself, or say out loud, "I am a child of God. As God shows me compassion, I can show compassion to myself."

Compassion is the ability to see how it all is.
— RAM DAS

If you have bought into the principles of the first three meditations, that God is compassionate and so we, in imitation of God,
must also be compassionate to everyone and everything, including
ourselves, you still need to know where all this compassion is
supposed to come from. We could say that it is simply within us,
like any other emotion or feeling. And as with any other emotion,
we can just wait for it to show up on its own, or we can work
toward its creation in our lives.

Today's quote suggests that it is as simple (and as difficult) as
seeing things as they really are. Most of the time we see things as we
want or expect them to be. Perhaps that is part of the human
condition. We all have lenses through which we look out into
reality. But when we see things as they are, we see them complete
with their faults and blemishes, their goodness and their strivings.
We see ourselves in the same way. This is the beginning of
compassion.

Place your hand on your heart. Feel its beating. With each beat,
imagine compassion being sent out into the universe, to all people,
to all living things.

Compassion is the chief law of human existence.
— FYODOR DOSTOYEVSKY

Judaism understands that God rules the world with a twin scale.
On one side is justice and on the other is compassion. If God used
compassion alone, there would be total anarchy in the world, for
we would know we could get away with anything. On the other
hand, if God used justice alone, none of us could survive the
scrutiny. But the scales are not evenly balanced; they are weighted
on the side of compassion.

We need such consideration, for after all, we are human. And to
be human is to fail, to not live up to others' expectations of us, to
not even live up to our own. God understands this. And so must we.

In our judgment of the world, we need to have a larger measure of compassion than anything else.

Imagine your own scales, the ones you use to evaluate yourself and others. Imagine the scales tipped to the side of compassion.

Even when angry, remember compassion, for You know our desires and inclinations. Remember that we are only dust.

— SELICHOT PRAYER

We do not pretend that we are perfect or without fault. After all, from whom can we hide our deficiencies? God knows what we are. We take responsibility and throw ourselves at the mercy of the court. This ownership is a key ingredient to our wholehearted return. And so long as we continue to act and think otherwise, we will stay locked in the prison of ourselves. This is true of our relationship with others and of our relationship with God. We need not pretend. We only need accept ourselves and ask for compassion.

Can you accept yourself? Can you ask for God's compassion? Then do it. Say to God, "I am only dust. Please have compassion on me." Say it every day, any day.

❧ ❧ ❧

m e d i t a t i o n s
HUMILITY

Each human being is often referred to as a small world. The way this is understood is this: If a person sees himself as "small" in his own vision, then he is, in fact, a "world." But if a person sees himself as a "world" in his own vision, then he is, in fact, "small."

— RABBI NOAH LEKHIVITZER

It begins with our self-perception. And because it is self-perception, only our internal monitors can help us check this one out.

How do you see yourself, honestly, now? Have you become large in your own eyes? Have your accomplishments and success gone to your head? Do you feel a sense of entitlement? Only you can answer these questions. Only you know if you have begun to see yourself as a world.

Say to yourself, "I am small." Look at yourself in the mirror and say it again. Say it until you really believe it. Repeat it as often as necessary.

A person should go through life with two slips of paper, one in each pocket. On the one in the left pocket should be written, "The world was created for my sake"; on the one in the right, "I am but dust and ashes."

— HASIDIC TEACHING

Humility, true humility, is not about self-deprecation. I remember as a boy watching my idol, Sandy Koufax, pitch a no-hitter. After the game he said in the interview, "I was pretty lucky today." I shouted at the television screen, "No you weren't! You were great!" I think we were both right. He was great that day, and I wanted him to take a little credit. He understood that both his fame and skill were fleeting, dependent, in part, on the team around him. Dust and ashes. And so it goes.

When we feel too full of ourselves, we ought to take out the note in our right pocket. And when we are down on ourselves, the left one is an excellent reminder. We need both.

So write yourself two notes today. Stick them in your pockets, or purse, or hold them, one in each hand. Be aware of the two messages and the balance they bring as you go about your business this, and every, day.

There is no room for God in the one who is full of himself.
— TEN RUNGS, MARTIN BUBER

That does not describe any of us, right? Certainly no one reading this book. We are all spiritual, the ones who are into this God thing. Of course, it sounds ridiculous when we hear it like this, but don't we sometimes feel that way, even if we do not admit it out loud?

One of the traps of the spiritual path is believing that somehow we are special because we are on it. *That* is being full of ourselves. And that leaves no room for God. When we sense the absence of God in our lives, the first question we need to ask ourselves is, "Have I created any room for the Holy One to enter?" Ask yourself, "Where is there room for God in my life?" Touch that place and breathe God in.

Do not be sure of yourself until the day of your death.
— PIRKE AVOT 2:5

So you have been reading this book, doing the meditations, and just as you were feeling good about yourself you crashed. Or, nothing happened. Same old person you always were, with the same old problems. And you thought this year was going to be different. This year you were going to make an honest effort and early start. So what went wrong?

Simply stated, what went wrong is that you thought you had it right. You thought you were totally sure and under contol. The spiritual journey is not made on a four-lane highway, with cruise control. While there very well may be bursts of movement, sudden awarenesses, and surprising leaps forward, especially when we are beginning a new discipline, most of our journeys are made on a winding, curved path which circles back on itself, even while it progresses forward. Certainty is a difficult commodity. It's like the book of theology the cartoon character Snoopy once was writing—*Did It Ever Occur To You, You Might Be Wrong?*

What are the things you are "sure of?" Write them down. Are you really sure?

It is better to deserve honors and not have them, than to have them and not deserve them.

— MARK TWAIN

So much of our lives is spent seeking recognition and approval from others. In part, this is what growing up is all about. We begin to define ourselves by what others think of us. But there comes a point at which reliance on the accolades of others can be negative, even destructive. No one knows who we are better than ourselves. We know what we deserve, and we know when what we get is superfluous. We can survive the disappointment of not getting what we think we deserve, but the distortions and expectations that come along with undeserved honors can be most harmful. We don't need them.

Think about the recognition that has come your way that you truly deserve. Now let it go. Think about what you have received that you really did not deserve. Now give it back. That's right. Give it back. It really isn't yours anyway.

Those who think they can live without others are wrong. But those who think others cannot survive without them are even more in error.

— HASIDIC FOLK SAYING

I remember my first year of teaching high school. I refused to take a day off because I just could not imagine how "my" kids could learn what I had to teach them without me. And then in my second year, I had a family crisis that required my being away for a couple of days. When I came back to class, I found they were still there. My substitute had followed my lesson plans and everyone was fine. I think they missed me—or at least some of them were kind enough to say so—but they had gotten along without me. Discovering that you are expendable is a tremendously humbling experience. It is also quite liberating. Yes, we matter. Yes, the world is different because we are part of it. Nevertheless, the world and those in it will survive without us. Thank God!

Think about the world without you in it. Imagine the ones you love going on with their lives. Though there is bound to be some sadness associated with this thought, see if you can find the place inside yourself that says it is okay. That sees the blessing that is there, as well.

FALL

NATURE OF GOD

O, my God! How does it happen in this poor old world that Thou art so great and yet nobody finds Thee; that Thou callest so loudly and nobody hears Thee; that Thou art so near and nobody feels Thee; that Thou givest to everybody and nobody knows Thy name?

— HANS DENK

This is the primary reality of the universe. God is everywhere, and somehow we fail to get it. It was voiced by our patriarch Jacob as he awoke from his sleep and called out, "Surely God is in this place, and I, I did not know it!" (Genesis 28:16), and it has been voiced by every great spiritual leader, every spiritual path ever since. There is no place devoid of God. Jacob needed to go to sleep in order to wake up to that truth. Others have found it through prayer, meditation, unexpected encounters, nature, God's revelation, simple acts of loving kindness, study, even a bush that burned unconsumed in the desert. God is with us, always at our side, wherever we may happen to be. We cannot see or touch this God, but we can feel the presence of the Holy One whenever we invite Him/Her in.

Close your eyes. Ask God to be with you. Use your own words. This is a request that God cannot deny.

Return unto Me and I will return unto you.

— MALACHI 3:7

Your move. God waits. Perhaps you think that is not fair. Why shouldn't God make the first move? After all, the stories of the Bible are replete with God having done just that. You may think, "Why should I have to make the first move?" If you feel this way, then don't. Perhaps you will be one of the "fortunate" ones that God will choose. So wait. But you do not have to. If you go up the mountain, God will come down; if you go out into the wilderness, God will meet you there; if you take a step in the right direction, God will walk toward you; if you reach up or out, God will grab your hand and pull you the rest of the way. That is God's certain promise. The journey begins with us.

So what are you waiting for? It does not matter how far away you have gone, or what you have gotten into. Return to God, and the Holy One will return to you. Today. Now. And whenever you feel separate and apart. Make any physical movement—take a step, stretch out your arms, bow your head, move your wheelchair forward: whatever works for you to symbolize your effort to return.

If we crave to have God in our lives, then we must purge ourselves of all that separates us from God.
— RABBI JOSEPH SOLOVEITCHIK

Many times I have had individuals come to my study who are truly seeking to have a sense of God in their lives, but deem themselves to be "not spiritual." They want to know what they have to do in order to feel close to God, because according to their own understanding, they have never had such an experience. I begin by exploring with them what their experiences have been. Sometimes it is a matter of definition. One might be expecting a loud voice from the heavens, and all the while fail to hear the still, small voice that has been broadcasting from within.

We then begin to examine patterns of behavior that may be

causing a separation. There are God-denying behaviors, actions that tend to push God away. Any unholiness tends to create in us, and around us, a barrier to God's presence. It is as if God simply cannot stand to be in a place of spiritual pollution. My teacher Rabbi David Ellenson told me that his mother taught it to him this way: "Act like the type of person God would choose as a friend." Good advice.

If you are feeling distance from God, take a look at how you are living your life. Take a good look. What are you doing, thinking, or feeling that may be causing a barrier to the closeness you seek?

Our idea of God tells us more about ourselves than about Him.
— THOMAS MERTON

There is nothing we can say about God with absolute certainty. All we have is partial understanding or awareness, and metaphor. Moses, God's servant par excellence, wants to know God completely. He asks, "Let me see Your face." To see one's face is to look into her/his eyes, to know who s/he is. God replies, "You cannot see me while still living. But I will show you *acharai*." *Acharai* is usually translated as "my back," but I think a better definition is "where I have been." We can see evidence of God's presence in the world. We can see where God has been. The rest is our imagery, our language, and that goes to the core of who we are. While this might be helpful in our conversations about God, it may or may not be saying anything about the Holy One.

What is your idea of God? Whatever it is, think of it as a mirror. What does it tell you about yourself?

God dwells in the details.
— ABY MORITZ WARBURG

So many people are searching for the big moment. We travel to all kinds of places, seeking experiences and teachers who can show us the way. If only the sky would open up, a sea part, the sun stand still. We need a miracle. Did you ever wonder how Moses knew the bush was burning unconsumed in the desert? A bush burning in a desert like Sinai is not particularly unusual; because of the high temperatures, that kind of thing happens frequently. The rabbis say he was off looking for a lamb that had separated himself from the rest of the flock. Having found the lamb, he stopped to watch the bush. It was only then that he realized it was not burning up. You have to take a really good look to notice something like that. And it was after that that God decided to be revealed to Moses.

There are so many burning bushes all around us. A flower growing on a hillside, a child laughing while at a playground, a homeless person waiting to clean your car window—details. When was the last time you stopped to notice?

> For Judaism, God is not a Kantian idea but an elementally present spiritual reality which religious man steadfastly confronts and non-religious man evades.
>
> — MARTIN BUBER

Either there is God who is the creative energy of the universe, or there is not. Those are our only two choices. God made us, or we made up God. Place your bets and live accordingly. We can do this consciously or unconsciously, but do it we must. Most people, even while saying they do believe, live as if there is no God. They have replaced God with an ideology, a state, a cause, or themselves. They become the sole determinant in how they live their lives. And so they live without awe, without wonder, without a will greater than their own. And this is death.

But it does not have to be that way. We can choose God as an "elementally present spiritual reality," even if we do not understand completely what that means right now, and truly live. That choice is ours. And always has been. What will you choose?

meditations
PERFECTION

To be the height of perfection is a fault.
— YIDDISH FOLK SAYING

Have you ever noticed that every character in the Hebrew Bible is flawed? Abraham lies, Sarah is jealous, Jacob is a deceiver, King David commits adultery, and on and on. There are no perfect people in our Bible so that we'll be reminded that we, too, cannot be perfect. There is no perfection in this world. Judaism does not strive for perfection; the Torah is not a utopian work. It understands that given the human condition, we are bound to fail, sometimes. That is just the way it is. The insistence on "being perfect" is apt to diminish the real goodness we can create here on earth. And that is a fault. We have become perfection crazy, and it is killing us. What ever happened to "good enough"?

Do you beat yourself up when you are less than perfect? Why?

The height of intellect is distinguishing between the real and the impossible and acceptance of what is beyond one's power to change.
— SOLOMON IBN GABIROL

In central Wisconsin there is an Amish community known for its beautiful quilts. Once, when my wife and I were traveling there with some friends, we met a particularly gifted artist who told us that whenever the Amish begin a quilt, they purposely put a mistake in it. We asked, "Why?" and she replied, "To remind us that only God is perfect." We all need such reminders. We need to be reminded every day. We are human and that means we are imperfect. That is just the way it is. And while we are remembering, let us also remember that this applies to those around us as well. They are not perfect, either. We need to stop insisting (and silently expecting) that they be. To expect perfection is to expect the impossible. We need to reject that notion so that we can do the work to which we are truly called in this lifetime.

What impossible perfections are you trying to effect in your world? What are you neglecting (and who are you harming) because of it?

> *You cannot find redemption until you see the flaws in your own soul.*
>
> — AUTHOR UNKNOWN

Not only is perfection impossible for us, but assuming its existence is actually a hindrance to our growth. We need flaws, we need mistakes, we need trials and errors. It is these, as much as anything else, that propel us forward, that sharpen our perspective. It is not that we have to seek them out, not try our best, or fail on purpose. But rather than try to avoid them, to deny or run from them, we need to begin to see them as blessings, and thank God for them.

Think about your flaws. Don't think of them as negatives. Don't try to hide them away. Rather, today, thank God for them.

> *But creation is never called perfect; it will be our task to assist the Creator in perfecting the creation, to become God's co-worker.*
>
> — DAVID ELLCOT

"And God looked at the entire creation and called the work very good." Not perfect. Very good. That is the way the Torah begins. And it has been our task, ever since, to continue the work and move it toward its completion. That is why we can say, "*hamotzi lechem min ha'aretz*/who brings forth bread from the earth." No one has ever seen a bread growing out of the earth. God brings forth wheat; it is we who turn it into bread. The blessing anticipates the completion of the work by human hands. We are God's partners and so the Holy One gets some of the credit.

Judaism understands that so long as we are human, the world will be imperfect and incomplete. That is the human condition. And so as long as we are alive, our work as God's partners never ends. But it imagines a time in which the world will be perfected. That is the time of the Messiah. Not our time. Not human time. A time in which all the rules as we know them will be suspended. In the meantime, we continue our work.

What are you doing to fulfill your role as God's coworker? How are you bringing about the completion of the world?

Jewish thought pays little attention to inner tranquility and peace of mind. The feeling of "behold, I've arrived" could well undermine the capacity to continue, suggesting as it does that the Infinite can be reached in a finite number of steps. In fact, the very concept of the Divine as Infinite implies an activity that is endless, of which one must never grow weary.
— RABBI ADIN STEINSALTZ

I often tell seekers, "If you want tranquility, Judaism is not the best way to get there." For how can we be tranquil in a world still waiting to be redeemed? The spiritual path is a journey, not a destination. There is no beginning and no end, just a path. We moderns are so used to the idea of setting goals and striving to realize them that we want to do the same with our spiritual goals.

We are willing to work hard, even for a long period of time, but we want to know when we will get there. But there is no "there"; only here. And wherever you go, you are always here. Perhaps our recognition of that reality can bring us some peace of mind. And so long as that merely strengthens us to continue on our way, no harm is done.

Try to picture the Infinite. Not a sky or an ocean, for those have a definite shape, with borders and boundaries. The Infinite. Imagine your place in the Infinite. That is where you are.

If someone tells you, "I tried but I did not achieve," do not believe him.

— TALMUD, MEGILLAH 6B

Trying is achieving. In fact, it is the only achievement we have. Again, if we imagine the spiritual journey as someplace at which we need to arrive someday (and the sooner the better), we will not get the truth of today's message. We will see all our efforts as falling short of some illusionary goal, and we will always feel as if we have not really achieved. But when we understand all of our lives, every minute of them, as works in progress, a progression that never ends, then we will be able to appreciate all the achievements along the way.

Think of all that you have already achieved in your lifetime. Give yourself the praise and credit you truly deserve.

~ ~ ~

meditations
TRUTH

And now here is my secret, a very simple secret: It is only with the heart that one can see rightly; what is essential is invisible to the eye.

— ANTOINE DE SAINT EXUPÉRY, THE LITTLE PRINCE

The High Holy Days of the Jewish people are (more than anything else) about seeing the world and ourselves "rightly." Practically all summer long we prepare ourselves for these days of judgment, a word we needn't be afraid of using. For what is judgment but seeing the world "rightly"? Now, as these days draw near, it is time to be honest, especially with ourselves. There can be nothing to hide now. Whom are we going to fool, anyway? And to what end? God sees all and our hearts know.

So let's look with our hearts; to see what is essential, what is most important, valuable. This is the moment of truth.

When you look at yourself and your life with your heart, what do you see?

There is a folk saying that truth travels all over the world. What is meant by this is that truth is banished from one place after another, and it therefore must wander all over the world.

— BA'AL SHEM TOV

Why are we so afraid of the truth? Why is it so difficult to find? What are we protecting? What is it we are defending against? Are we so fragile, our lives so delicately balanced, so held together by deception and dishonesty that we cannot bear the light of truth?

What a relief it would be if we could just be honest with ourselves and those whose lives intersect with our own. We could stop all the games we play and the roles we take on, trying to be someone we think we are supposed to be, someone we think they want us to be, someone we think they would love. Instead, we are like truth itself: wandering the earth, never quite feeling at home, never finding the peace of simply being who and what we are.

Is this what you really want? Is this how you want to spend your life? Or is it time to stop truth's exile, at least from your own life? Why don't you call truth back? Take the risk. What are you waiting for?

Truth and justice, kindness and truth. This means that truth is without effect if not accompanied by justice and kindness.

— REUBEN ALCALAY

I think the modern version of the above quote's wisdom is Paul Simon singing, "You don't have to lie to me, just give me some tenderness beneath your honesty." We think the truth has to be brutal. And perhaps that is one of the reasons we refrain from seeking it in our lives, speaking it to others. But the choices are not a lie on the one hand or hurtful truth on the other. Truth can be accompanied by kindness (concern for the other) and justice (doing the right thing). In fact, if it is not, it would be better off not said. Honesty for honesty's sake can be quite destructive. We have to be very careful when unleashing this powerful force in the world.

What truth have you been carrying around that you would like to reveal but have not as yet? Is it out of concern for yourself, or for another? Can you find a way to bring justice and kindness into the picture? If you can, this might be the time to do so.

Not to deceive another person is mandated by law. The pious person also refrains from self-deception.
                                              — KOTZKER REBBE

Deception is clearly a negative. It encases us in a world in which we are always having to cover our tracks, trying to remember what we said, lying to cover up other lies, making our lives just plain miserable. Some of us learned to lie because of the temporary advantage it seemed to give us over the other; others of us learned to lie because we did not feel worthy of receiving whatever it is we wanted or needed. And so began a life of sneaking around and telling others what we wanted them to know, or what we thought they wanted to know.

But why do we deceive ourselves? Are we even aware that we do? Can self-deception be premeditated? I don't think so. To not deceive ourselves takes a great deal of self-reflection. It is the desire to carefully consider our words and our actions, even our beliefs. It requires a great deal of self-awareness, of knowing who and what we are, and behaving accordingly. It is a matter of wanting to make sure that we harmonize our outer and inner selves. It is saying what we mean, and meaning what we say. It is an act of piety, because all the action is internal, and so are the rewards. We do not receive any attention or accolades for doing this work.

Not to deceive does not mean we must reveal everything. It just means we have to stop lying, to others and to ourselves. Are you deceiving anyone? Are you deceiving yourself? What would it take to stop?

Both this view and that view are the words of the living God.
                                              — TALMUD, ERUVIN 13B

What kind of God would it be who allowed us only one flavor of the truth? Judaism has long recognized that even differing opinions can both be the words of God, that both can be true. That is one of the reasons dissenting opinions are published side by side in the Talmud and Midrash. That we may believe one or the other could just be a product of our limitations, saying nothing about the inherent truth of what we have heard or read. Truth is like light in a spectrum. We see only a small band of it, but we know there are other colors out there. I do not deny their existence based on my limitations.

What truth that someone else has expressed to you have you had trouble accepting? Just because s/he said it does not mean it is true, but are you willing to ask yourself this question: Can there be any truth in what this person is saying to me? It is a good question to keep in mind whenever you are speaking to another. (It was taught to me by psychotherapist Ted Bruce.)

I am Adonai, your God . . . True.

— DAILY PRAYERBOOK

By tradition, the ending of the *v'ahavtah* is linked to the prayer that comes immediately after it, the *geulah,* forming a phrase not intended by the prayer book itself. By reciting them this way, they become a declaration of faith and commitment—It is true that Adonai is your God. Adonai and only Adonai is our God. This is an important realization, especially before the High Holy Days. In fact, these holidays make little sense unless we can say, "Adonai is our God." This is the ultimate truth of the universe. There is one God. The challenge, as always, is to make that God our own.

Are you able to declare that Adonai is your God? Is that true for you? Are you willing to say it, even if you are uncertain right now? Try it. "I am Adonai, your God . . . True."

ROSH
haShanah/
Yom Kippur and
The Ten Days
of Awe

～

Rosh haShanah and Yom Kippur are bookends holding up eight days in between them (for a total of ten days of awe). On Rosh haShanah we recognize that God is central to our lives by proclaiming God as Sovereign and Parent. On Yom Kippur we come before that God to fully disclose what we have done and who we are, accepting God's judgment as to whether or not we are worthy of another year of life.

meditations

Ten Days of Awe

• Day One •

Came to believe that a Power greater than ourselves could restore us to sanity.
> — Twelve Steps of Alcoholics Anonymous

Some of the most spiritual work being done today is through Twelve Step programs. Perhaps it has something to do with going to the very bottom of ourselves. At the core of the Twelve Steps is the recognition of a Higher Power. Unless and until we accept this Higher Power in our lives, all our attempts to free ourselves of whatever addictions we have—alcohol, drugs, sex, gambling, workaholism, perfectionism, consumerism—will be in vain.

Rosh Hashanah is a coronation ceremony. On Rosh Hashanah we name God "King of Kings," accepting God as our Higher Power. God and only God. Rosh Hashanah helps us shift our focus from an anthropocentric (human-centered) to a theopocentric (God-centered) universe. It is only through getting ourselves out of the center that we can find true balance and wholeness in our lives. Draw a circle. That circle is your life. At the very center of that circle, write the letter G. How would your life be different if God was really in the center?

〜〜 〜〜 〜〜

• Day Two •

A new year has begun, reminding us of the eternal possibility of renewal.

— EUGENE KOHN

Renewal. To be new. To begin again. To not be held back by past mistakes, errors, flaws, sins. What a powerful notion. What powerful medicine against beating ourselves up with blame, complacency, defeatism. A new year. Anything is possible.

And it begins with letting go of the past. Forgiveness is the task. To forgive ourselves and to forgive others who have hurt and wronged us. Not to forget. But to forgive. To let ourselves and them begin again. And even if there are those who will not forgive us, we can begin the process. We can forgive.

Make a list of the things for which you would like to be forgiven. Whenever possible, ask those you have wronged for their forgiveness. Make this the year in which you tell others that you forgive them.

~ ~ ~

• Day Three •

As one should say a blessing for every good fortune, so one should for every misfortune.

— Talmud, Berachot 48b

Saying "Thank you, God" comes easily to our lips when things are going right in our world. It is a normal, natural act of gratitude. But for our misfortunes? Does the Talmud really expect that we should be grateful for all the terrible things that happen in our lives? Isn't this masochism?

Blessings can be many things. Some can express our hopes and dreams; some can express our gratitude; but every blessing recognizes that God is in there in all things. Even the bad things. Even the terrible moments when we feel all alone, abandoned by others, abandoned by God. It is precisely at these moments that we need to say a *bracha*/blessing recognizing God's role, not necessarily in causing these things to happen to us, but in being there to hold us and to see us through. And in some measure, though in the moment of misfortune we can rarely see it, we need to realize that this, too, will lead us to grow and deepen, to become the person we are yet to be.

Think of all the bad things that happened to you this year. See if you can bless God for them, one at a time.

· Day Four ·

You need to claim the events of your life to make yourself yours.
— ANN WILSON SCHAEF

Everything that happens to us, is us. There are so many times
when we want to deny this, to blame others, to pretend it never
happened, to distance ourselves from the ugliness we may have
been a part of. There are other times when we cannot accept our
success. We downplay our goodness, we slough off our accomplishments, we fail to take credit when it is due, we do not allow others
to be grateful for what we have done. Both the negative and the
positive, as well as all the moments in between—that is our life.
And in order for us to be wholly and truly ourselves, we will need
to take responsibility for it all.

Think about the things you have done this year for which you
have yet to claim credit. Write out a claim check for each one, and
when you are ready, go and "pick them up."

~~ ~~ ~~

· Day Five ·

Rabbi Isaac Luria began his evening prayer by reciting, "I hereby forgive whoever has sinned against me this day."
— 100 Blessings Every Day, Rabbi Kerry Olitzky

We had a rule in my house when we were growing up. We were never allowed to go to bed angry at any other member of our family. Whatever it was, no matter how badly one wronged or hurt us, we had to forgive or ask forgiveness before we went to bed. I did not always feel like doing that. I even remember feeling resentful at times for having to say "I accept your apology" when I was still hurting, but I did it. And you know what? I still do it to this day.

There is something very cleansing about not holding on to a resentment for longer than a day. When we take it to bed with us, it grows, and becomes more difficult to carry or release. We tend to dig in our heels deeper and deeper the longer we hold on to it, defending our position, becoming more self-protective, even more self-righteous. Hence Rabbi Luria's rule: No more than one day.

Consider all the things you have been holding on to for more than one day. All the people you have yet to forgive for wrongs they perpetrated against you more than a single day ago. Will this be the day you forgive them?

• Day Six •

We do not ask that our past sins be forgiven in the sense that their effects may be canceled . . . All we can do and ask for is better insight, purer faith, fuller strength.

— CLAUDE G. MONTEFIORE

Let us be clear on one thing: Every sin we commit (and I define sin as anything that we do or say that moves us away from God) has an effect on us and others. Asking for forgiveness does not change what we may have done or said. Asking for forgiveness does not mean it never happened. Our deeds and words may have wounded or scarred others. They may have damaged us in the process. These hurts are real and can be long-lasting, even permanent. Asking for forgiveness does not negate our responsibility.

But it does say we are sorry. That we wish it never happened. And that we will strive to never repeat this sin again. That is the best we can do. In the interim, we hope that we grow from the pain we have caused so that we will have better insight, fuller strength, and the faith in ourselves to refrain from causing this hurt again.

What sins have you committed this year? What insights have you gained as a result?

~ ~ ~

• Day Seven •

*For who so forgives is forgiven in turn; hardheartedness and a
temper that will not make up quarrels are a heavy burden of sin,
and unworthy of an Israelite.*

— MOSES OF COUCY

Forgiving is not easy, especially when we were unjustly wronged
or wounded. Children of parental abuse, abandoned spouses,
workers who are "downsized," the "unfavored" child, elderly who
are "warehoused" by their children . . . many of us have legiti-
mate reasons to be hurt and angry. Righteous indignation is often
the most appropriate response we can have. And our tradition does
tell us to "hate evil." But the irony of holding on to these feelings
and not forgiving those who wronged us is that we get hurt a
second time. Refusal to forgive is a sin against the self. We can do
better.

These ten days are an opportunity to finally forgive those who
sinned against us. It does not cancel the effects of their actions, but
it does allow us to get on with our lives. Think of the people you
have yet to forgive. Will this be the day you forgive them?

~ ~ ~

· Day Eight ·

*You cannot find redemption until you see the flaws in your own
soul.*

— MARTIN BUBER

There are times when others truly hurt and/or offend us. They
need to ask for our forgiveness, and we need to find the place in our
hearts to forgive. But there are other moments when our pain is
caused by a self-righteousness that sees the flaws and shortcomings
in others, but not in ourselves. We are quick to point out their
failures, their inabilities, their weaknesses, and while these may
very well be there, our redemption will not come about by
observing them; rather it will come only by seeing ourselves, clearly
and deeply. In fact, looking outward is often an escape from the
work we need to do.

This is the season for looking within, for being honestly self-
critical. As you look inside today, what flaws do you see in your
own soul?

⌣ ⌣ ⌣

• Day Nine •

Rabbi Nachman of Bratzlav interpreted the verse in Psalms 38:19, "I admit my sin; I worry about my transgression," as meaning that ruminating about old mistakes and about the past can in itself be sinful.
— LIVING EACH DAY, RABBI ABRAHAM TWERSKI

It has been said that in order to be truly human, one has to have a bad memory. There comes a point that our dwelling on the past, beating ourselves up for our transgressions, is self-destructive. We are all sinners. That is part of the human condition. We sin because we are imperfect. Imperfect people make mistakes. Sometimes those mistakes are awful, hurting the very ones we love the most, leaving permanent scars. Sometimes the mistakes are careless or even inadvertent—a word of gossip, a moment of weakness or selfishness, a little looking out for number one, an opportunity not taken, a hardening of our hearts. There are a myriad of moments when we should have done or said something other than what we did. We sin. We own those sins, sincerely ask for forgiveness, and try to do better. Really try. That is the best we can do.

So which old mistakes are you still holding on to? Will this be the year you let go of them and get on with your life?

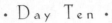

· Day Ten ·

For I have come to know your truth; I accept your judgments
upon me; And am content with my life.
— THE DEAD SEA SCROLLS

Yom Kippur is a rehearsal for our own death. We dress in a white
kittel (which reminds us of burial shrouds), we light a twenty-four-
hour *yahrzeit* candle that connects us to those we have loved and
reminds us of our own mortality, we abstain from food and liquid,
we attend little to bodily functions or pleasures (no shaving, no
makeup, no bathing, etc.), and we pray a liturgy that focuses us on
the content and meaning of our lives, all in an attempt to feel what
it might be like when we are dead. And so that we may learn to
accept ourselves, accept our lives, accept all that befalls us and be
content. Death is the ultimate acceptance, for it is the ultimate limit,
God's judgment on each of us. If we can learn to accept our death,
then we can learn to accept our lives as well.

Self-acceptance is a process that takes many years. These High
Holy Days invite us to take a giant step in that direction. Are you
ready to do so?

~ ~ ~

meditations

I AM ALIVE!
(FOR THE FOUR DAYS
AFTER YOM KIPPUR)

Yom Kippur is not eating, not sleeping much, not having sex, not dressing in fine clothes, and looking in the mirror and seeing what you're going to look like after you've died. And the most joyous noise a Jew can hear is the sound of the shofar announcing the end of Yom Kippur, because it means that you have lived through the day of death and not died.
— RABBI LAWRENCE KUSHNER

After all the hard work of being honest with ourselves, admitting and owning our sin failures, asking for forgiveness and resolving in *t'shuvah* to change our lives, we come to recognize that ultimately it is beyond our control. Yom Kippur is the Day of Judgment. On this day, God made final judgment on our lives. We did everything we could. We came to Yom Kippur dressed in our symbolic shrouds (the *kittel*) saying we were ready to accept God's decree for us. Now it is up to God.

The fact that you are reading this means you have been granted another day. What will you do with it? How much of Yom Kippur's message will remain with you as you go back to work? How will you reinforce your resolve? What will get you there? Who will be your partners and helpers? How will you forgive yourself when you fail? Don't wait for next Yom Kippur to answer these questions. Begin to formulate your answers today, and every day.

What is a day in a person's life? Isn't it the most precious treasure that can be given us?

           — Morris Goldstein

Another day. That is the way they come to us, one day at a time. The workout begins with the *Modeh,* a prayer of gratitude for another day of life. There is no assumption that we will get this gift or that we deserve it. Our tradition has us take on the posture of grateful surprise each and every morning when we wake up. "Oh wow! I am alive! *Modeh ahni* . . . Thank you, thank you, God, for having enough faith and trust in me that you gave me another day. You are incredible!" And so it is up to us, no matter what our profession, to make the most of this day and to see the multitude of opportunities each day grants us to do God's work in the world. Speaking to our clients, taking care of our children's needs, beautifying our home environments, selling something that someone truly needs . . . it does not matter what the task. They can all be accomplished with a sense of *mitzvah,* a sense of urgency, a sense of gracious gift.

Another day. What will you do with this precious treasure that has been given you?

Wherever you go, God goes with you.

           — Devarim Rabbah 2:10

Remember how close to God you felt . . . was it just two days ago? Perhaps it was coming together with other Jews? Or was it the music? Could it have been the words of the liturgy? Did you hear them for what seemed to be the first time this year? Did the emptiness of your body fill you with a sense of the Holy? Or was it a combination of all these things?

In a sense, it is easy to feel close to God on a day like Yom Kippur, a day in which we give ourselves over to the task of inner focus and expression. But Judaism does not contain many days like this, because it wants us to be a part of life and its tasks. That is why it is essential that we remember that there is no place devoid of God, if only we let the Holy One in. Throughout your day (and every day) when you feel yourself alone and on your own, remind yourself that God is with you. There is no place you can go that God will not go with you.

> Our whole program of Jewish living is to help us to become articulate and express our wonder as we stand in awe before God.
>
> — ABRAHAM E. HALPERN

If we change the syllables in the words "Day of Atonement," it can become "Day of At-one-ment." For after all, isn't that what Yom Kippur is really all about? No matter how far we have drifted or strayed, no matter how many marks we have missed, God invites us back to full and total relationship. Our t'shuvah/return is said to be complete on this day. We and God are truly one. The trick is to stay conscious of that the other 364 days of the year.

We do not need miracles for that to happen. A simple brachal blessing before we eat a piece of food will do it. And if you do not know the traditional one, just make one up: "Thank you, God, for providing us with these strawberries." If blessings for food seem awkward (if you can say them in restaurants, you can say them anywhere), how about going outside each day and pausing to take in the sunshine, the clouds in the sky, a body of water, a star twinkling? You can look at the face of your lover, your child, or a coworker. You can stop to say hello to the homeless man you pass on your way to work, or better yet, bring him a sandwich. You can do this workout. In every act, or any act, look at the wonder of God's creation, and say, "Oh, wow!" Make that your goal for this year—say "Oh, wow!" and mean it, at least once a day.

SUKKOT

~

Sukkot works on two levels. As an agricultural festival, it calls on us to demonstrate our gratitude to God, who has provided the harvest for us. As a historical holy day, it reminds us of our wilderness wanderings, when we dwelt in temporary housing and were dependent on God for our survival. By building a sukkah and "dwelling" in it (taking meals there, camping out, etc.), we reenact this experience so that we can sense this reliance on God. In our modern, settled society, we especially need these reminders. On the personal level, Sukkot is a time of maturity in which we reap the harvest of our own work in the world.

~   ~   ~

meditations
SIMCHA/JOY

When we share with others, their joy becomes ours.
— RABBI ABRAHAM TWERSKI

One of the great customs of the Sukkot holiday is called *ushpizin,* the invitation of guests, both mythical and human, into our sukkahs. Each night, we share food, drink, and conversation with others as we sit under the stars enjoying these beginning days of fall. Before the hibernation of winter gets under way, we share our joy with others, both strangers and friends.

Sharing is an opening of self, a generosity of spirit. It is a kind of self-confidence. We have just reaped our harvest. We have much to give, to share with others. It is this sharing that gives us a feeling of joy. And when we share in this manner, we feel the joy of others as well.

At this time of harvest, sense your fullness, your completeness. Take a good look at all that you have—your material and spiritual blessings. It is time to share and feel the joy of doing so.

In your love, Adonai our God, You have given us festivals for rejoicing, holy days, and times of gladness, this Sukkot festival, the time of our joy, to remember our exodus from Egypt.
— FESTIVAL PRAYERBOOK

The word "holiday" is really made up of two words, "holy" and "day." "Holy" (*kadosh* in Hebrew) means to separate, to keep apart. We need holy days, otherwise our lives would be a drudgery, all work and no play, with no opportunity to focus on our higher calling, our deeper sense of ourselves and our place in this world. That is why we are doing this workout. And that is why it is only ten minutes long. Because in the normative course of our days we do not give ourselves that much time to focus on our spirit and its needs. But on holy days we can. They are gifts from God in that they remind us to stop what we are usually doing, and take time for our inner selves.

More than any other holiday, Sukkot is associated with joy. The harvest is over. It is party time. In the ancient world, this meant a pilgrimage to Jerusalem—a weeklong holy day to give expression to our feeling of joy. I get the sense in our own time that there are lots of parties, even more free time, but very little joy.

What is the joy you are feeling right now? How will you express it?

Some people are afraid to enjoy the present because they anticipate that their happiness will soon come to an end. They create their own misery either by worrying about their past or by being anxious about the future, both of which are beyond their control. In this way they forfeit the joy of the present.

— REBBE NACHMAN OF BRATZLAV

It is one of the great truths of life that we all (sometimes) forget. This moment is all there is. The past is over; we can learn from it but cannot do anything about it. The future is only a promise; we can plan and prepare but we have no guarantee it will ever arrive. All we have for sure is now. We can live that now. We can throw ourselves fully and wholly into it. Squeeze out of it all we can. Experience and savor every moment. And from it, derive all the joy that is possible.

Not every moment in life is pleasant. Sadness and pain also constitute a part of each of our existences. But there is much joy in the moment if we are willing and able to really live it. Are you deriving the joy that is yours? Or are you missing some because you are too focused on the past or worried about the future? What will it take for you to let go of what was or that which is yet to be?

Weeping may stay for the night, but joy comes in the morning.

— PSALM 30:6

Sadness is a reality. It enters all of our lives and we should not deny it or fail to give it expression. The fully functioning, healthy adult knows how to be sad. And in the midst of our sadness we are likely to feel that it will engulf us, last forever. The psalmist comes to remind us then that with the dawning of a new day, joy will return to our lives. That is a certain promise. However, we need to know how to let go of the sadness, and move on with our lives. There will always be something for which we can be joyous. Always.

As you start this (and each) day list the things for which joy is your most appropriate response. If you are not feeling it, ask yourself why.

Serve God with joy; come before the One with gladness.
— PSALM 100:2

The word for service in Hebrew, *avodah,* is the same word that is used for the work of a slave, and, interestingly enough, it is the word the sages used for prayer. One way of imaging our relationship with God (not very popular these days) is that of master to slave. For us moderns, the whole institution of slavery is so abhorrent that conjuring it up in our minds is likely to fill us with revulsion, anger, and disgust. We think of the tortured experience of African-Americans, or of apartheid in South Africa, both shameful scars in the history of the world. And yet our rabbis, who were not so far removed from the experience of our own slavery in Egypt, chose this image for our relationship with God, even what it means to pray. Why?

The slavery of one human being to another will always be marred, because human beings were not created to have that kind of power over one another; it will always be abused. Our only true Master can be God. And when we come before this Master, whether it be to help another human being or to reconnect in prayer, it ought to fill us with joy. When we do God's work in the world, all relationships are as they are meant to be. Again, we ought to be filled with joy.

How did you come before God this morning in your workout blessings and prayers? How will you serve God the rest of this day?

Be open-eyed to the great wonders of nature, familiar though they may be. But people are more wont to be astonished at the sun's eclipse than at its unfailing rise.
— ORHOT TZADIKIM 15C

With all the human suffering and misery in the world, what is there to be joyous about? How about the sun rising? Yes, I know it happens every day, but does that not make it even more of a miracle? Yet we are more likely to denigrate it because of its regularity, perhaps not even notice it because it is a positive addition to our lives, to all of life. What is it about the human being that tends to take notice of things only when they are taken away? Is taking things for granted built into the genetic code of our humanity?

Joy is an antidote. Joy can help us to stay awake, to be alive to the wonder that is all of life. Look at all the things that are so very familiar—the view from your window, the tree on your block, the sun in the sky. Look at them as if you have never seen them before, and feel the joy of simply being alive.

* * *

The weeks between Sukkot and Chanukah are the longest stretch in the Hebrew calendar without a holiday. With the celebration of the harvest lasting as long as we can possibly make it (seven days, plus Sh'mini Atzeret, plus Simchat Torah—the latter two combined on the Reform and Israeli calendar), we return to our homes to make ready for winter, with its shorter days and colder weather. After our joyous days in the sukkah, it is time to turn inward and do some self-reflection.

meditations
GRATITUDE

If the only prayer you say in your whole life is "thank you," that would be enough.

— MEISTER ECKHART

We generally recognize three categories of prayer—praise of God and God's creation, petitions for the fulfillment of our needs and the needs of others, and gratitude to God for all that we have. Why would a simple "thank you" be enough, then? Because it would have recognized a basic premise—that we are recipients, that all we have is a gift. We live in a time in which most everyone feels a sense of entitlement. Ours is a rights-driven society. "Thank you" says the opposite. It is a confrontation between two notions of reality. "Thank you" is the beginning of the life of the spirit.

The first words out of a Jewish person's mouth as s/he awakes each day are supposed to be *modah/modeh*/thank you. Did you say it this morning? Thank you, God, for another day of life. Thank you.

Who is rich? One who has the ability to be happy with his/her lot in life.

— PIRKE AVOT 4:1

Someone said it to me this way: "If someone is not happy with what he already has, why does he think getting more would make him more happy?" Sounds pretty simple. And yet, don't we really behave as if our success and self-worth are dependent on how much we acquire, how big our salaries are, the house we live in, the art on the walls, the vacations we take, the cars we drive? Some two thousand years ago, the rabbis already understood that the acquisition syndrome ("more, more") would not only not lead to our happiness, but would drive us crazy.

It is the season of Sukkot. The time of harvest. Look around at what you have and be grateful for it. Say to yourself, "If I never add another thing to my closet or collections, I have enough. I am already blessed beyond my wildest dreams or imagination. Thank you, God." This is your meditation for this day. Thank God for what you already have "harvested" in life.

If you can't have what you want, want what you can have.
                    — SOLOMON IBN GABIROL

None of us can have what we want all of the time. Nor should we be able to. What we want is not always what we need, and at times, what we want can even be harmful to us. Sometimes, my children seem like "want machines"; my job, then, as a parent is to say a lot of noes, reminding them that just because they want something, does not mean they are going to get it. We are all, in this regard, children.

Wants are desires. Judaism teaches us that there is nothing wrong with having desires. But they need to be controlled, channeled, so that they do not drive us crazy. Matching our desires with what we can realistically and appropriately have is a key element in our developing a sense of gratitude in our lives. What do you want? What do you really want? Is it something you can have? If not, let it go.

When I wake up in the morning I thank God for all the little things in life; like waking up in the morning.
                    — AUTHOR UNKNOWN

The poet, e. e. cummings invited us to be grateful for all the "yes" in our lives, all the amazing, wonderful occurrences of everyday life.

There is so much "yes" in our lives. Each of our lives. If only we would remember to remember it. The problem is we get caught up in the negative moments, or try to evaluate, make a judgment about the all of it far too often. The task is to stay focused on the day, on the moment, to see what is around us, all around us. This *is* an amazing day! We are alive!

Take some time to really look at things today. See how amazing they are. Say it out loud! "Look at that amazing tree . . . Did you see that fantastic sunset? . . . I ate the best apple for lunch . . ."

If one sees a large crowd, one should thank God for not having made them all of one mind. For just as each person's face is different one from the other, so is each person's thoughts different from any other.

— TALMUD, BERACHOT 58A

Judaism does, in fact, have a blessing for everything. After all, our tradition enjoins us to say one hundred blessings every day. Can you imagine if you actually did that, if you truly thanked God for all the things that come your way each and every day? For every piece of food you ate, for every time you went to the bathroom, for the ability to think, for each of your senses, for the beauties of nature . . . The idea behind the hundred blessings is to raise our consciousness to the wonder that is life.

We are different, you and I. We spend so much fruitless energy trying to minimize differences, to get others to think and act like us. What a pity. What a waste of time. Instead, we could simply thank God for having made each of us different and unique. That is what makes life so rich, so interesting, so difficult and incredible.

Spend some time today thanking God for differences. Try to really mean it.

How well off we are! How good is our lot in life! How pleasant our destiny! How beautiful our inheritance!

— DAILY LITURGY

It has not always been so easy to make this declaration on a daily basis. For centuries it has seemed like our lot in life was to suffer simply because we were Jews. More than once has our people thought, "Why doesn't God choose someone else for a while?" Yet despite that, we continued to hold on to this *ashreinu* prayer as a kind of mantra. Unfortunately, because of childhood experiences, many of us came to see our Jewish inheritance (primarily) as a drudgery or a burden—loaded with responsibilities and negative memories. How often I have counseled someone who was wounded or shamed by a rabbi or Jewish teacher. Nevertheless, our tradition maintains that it is otherwise, that we are fortunate, the luckiest people on the planet. And indeed, what a wonderful treasure has been entrusted to us. If only we would seek it out, experience it, live it.

Think about all the things you love about being Jewish. Be grateful for them today.

❧ ❧ ❧

meditations

MIDLIFE EVALUATION

Please, O God, have mercy upon me that I should not live a life of futility. May I always reflect upon myself, "What am I doing in this world?"

— REBBE NACHMAN OF BRATZLAV

We have returned to our homes. The time of rejoicing is over. In many parts of the world, the leaves on the trees are turning colors. There is a coolness in the air, perhaps some frost on the ground. The days are getting shorter. Our year (which symbolically represents our lives) is half over. Winter, symbol of death, is approaching. This is the autumn of our lives, when we turn inside and ask ourselves, "What am I doing in this world? What is the meaning of my life? Why am I here? What difference do I make?" For some, it is a time of crisis. They run from the questions and desperately attempt to return to adolescence. In doing so, they (temporarily) escape from having to answer, often hurting their families and loved ones in the process. But the questions will not go away. And sooner or later, we will have to answer them. That is the nature of our lives. Youth is over. Old age is not yet upon us. This is the time of self-reflection.

So ask yourself, "What *are* you doing in this world? Why are you really here? And what *are* you doing about it?" Ask yourself, as if this is your last chance to do so.

And Adonai called to the man and asked, "Where are you?"
— GENESIS 3:9

Adam hears the question and tries to hide. But God is not asking in order to find out where Adam is, for the Holy One sees and knows all. God is asking for Adam's sake, so that he can come to terms with where he is in the world. This is a spiritual question.

Adam has eaten from the tree of knowledge of good and evil. Whether this was in disobedience to God's demand or the inevitable consequence of growing up is difficult to say. Nevertheless, Adam is no longer who he once was. And God wants to know what this change has done for him. Adam tries to avoid answering the question. He hides, as if one can hide from God. And then, found, he says, "The woman You gave me made me do it."

God asks us as well. Where are you? Where are you in this world? Will we try to hide, avoid answering? Or can we say, "Here I am"?

He who defines himself can't know who he really is.
— LAO-TZU

A definition is a box. Words can and need to be defined. Not people. Think about it. Only when a person's life is over do we put him or her in a box. To do so while s/he is living would be an act of murder.

Moses wants desperately to know God. He asks the Holy One, "Tell me Your name." But God responds, "I have many names and none of them are Me. I will be that which I will be . . . I will be." God is the act of always becoming. And to a large extent, so are we. We are like God in that respect. We cannot limit ourselves to a name, to an occupation, to an address, to a definition. Any attempt to do so (and we are always trying) will always be inaccurate, leaving out a part of who and what we are. It would be much better to share ourselves than to try to define those selves.

Be yourself today. Just be it. Without explanations or definitions. Take notice of the person you are.

A foolish consistency is the hobgoblin of little minds.
— RALPH WALDO EMERSON

As Walt Whitman once wrote, we are all large. And we all contain multitudes. Self-knowledge is not the same as consistency. We need not be consistent, at least not all of the time. To even attempt to be would be to deny parts of ourselves. Instead, we need to give expression to who and what we are, and learn about ourselves from that expression.

Often, someone will point out to me that one thing or another that I said or did contradicted a previous statement or action. They mean for me to clarify or to denounce one or the other action or statement. Obviously, they see the contradiction as a negative. I invariably respond, "Good," and then quote Emerson. I can be conflicted; I can have more than one opinion on a single topic; I can even be confused. Self-reflection is about coming to terms with who we are, not with someone else's idea or ideal about who and what we should be.

Are there aspects of yourself that are contradictory? Can you accept all sides without trying to rid yourself of one or the other?

On the second day, God created the angels, with their natural propensity to do good. Later, God made beasts with their animal desires. But God was pleased with neither. So God fashioned a human, a combination of angel and beast, free to follow good or evil.

— ISAAC OF CORBEIL

Perhaps this is an oversimplification—angel as the force for good and beast as the force for evil, animal desires—but I think the overall concept is not. We are, each of us, a battleground for good and evil. Many of us who grew up in modernity have rejected that notion. First of all, we don't like the thought that evil is real. Second, as inheritors of relativism, we are no longer sure about what is good. And even if it is good for me, it may not be good for you.

But our desire for self-knowledge and reflection will be thwarted unless and until we come to know, understand, accept, and (ultimately) control those forces within. In large measure, that is the major issue of our midlife.

See the goodness in yourself. Face the evil. How will you give expression to the former and control the latter?

There are three types of exile and they are of increasing severity. The first is when Jews are in exile among other nations, the second is when Jews are in exile among fellow Jews, and the third and most severe is when a Jew is alien to himself, for then he is both captor and captive, in exile within himself.

— RABBI SHOLOM ROKEACH OF BELZ

We will not discuss the first two types of exile here, though both are real and both are important. It is exile from self that concerns us at the moment. Many Jews in the twentieth century thought they could be citizens of the world. In the process, many shed their

Judaism altogether. Others thought they could wear their Judaism like an ornament, proudly taking it out whenever they wanted or needed it, then safely tucking it away when it was deemed irrelevant or inconvenient. Over time, they "took it out" less and less—special holidays and life-cycle events. But being Jewish is not about "stuff you have to do"; it is about "who you can be."

Yes, on occasion, a soul is born into the wrong body and the life's work of that soul will be to become someone else. That is what conversion is really all about. But most of the time, the problem is self-alienation, self-exile. Our tradition understands exile as a punishment worse than death. And so it is.

Midyear (midlife) is a time to recognize where we have gone, where we have gotten to. If we are in exile from ourselves, our Jewishness, it is time to come home. Are you ready to come home to yourself? Then what are you waiting for? If you are already on that path, acknowledge yourself for the steps you have taken thus far, or ask for this acknowledgment from another traveler.

meditations

BOREDOM

That which has been, it is that which shall be; and that which has been done, it is that which shall be done; and there is nothing new under the sun.

— ECCLESIASTES 1:9

Boredom is not a scheduling matter; it is a spiritual one. It comes from the expectation that what makes life good and interesting is a continual stream of new experiences, new people, new "toys." And this lust for what is new is none other than our subconscious attempt to prolong youth and avoid death. But autumn is here, the days are getting shorter, and winter's death is unavoidable, part of what makes us human—part of what makes life precious. This long stretch between Sukkot and Chanukah, this time known as *Mar Cheshvan*/bitter month of Cheshvan, is preparing us, readying us for winter and death. Boredom is one of the challenges along the way. There is nothing new, nothing that has not been said, nothing that has not been done before. We need to get that straight. And even if it feels new the first time, it will soon become a repetitive action. That is reality. Our challenge is to approach everything as if it were for the first time, the only time. For in truth, life comes to us one day at a time; we have not been here before, reading these words, at this moment, and we will never be here again.

Throughout your day, look at everything as if you have never been there before. Take in your surroundings, examine objects, really observe and listen to the people you encounter. By day's end, think about how approaching experience this way changes it, changes you. You will never be bored again.

> *As it is, we are merely bolting our lives—gulping down undigested experiences as fast as we can stuff them in—because awareness of our own existence is so superficial and so narrow that nothing seems to us more boring than simple being.*
> — ALAN WATTS

I think it begins with childhood. It is oftentimes more difficult for me to make an appointment to see a child than to see an adult. School is the least of it. My contemporaries seem bent on making sure their children do not have a free moment—sports, and lessons, and private tutors . . . Whatever happened to free time to just relax, to create one's own games, to interact with one's siblings, to talk about the day? My wife and I have established two rules in this regard—one extracurricular activity per child per semester, and everyone has to be home together for dinner. There is no television on during that time. When we share this with other couples, we get some very strange looks and lots of reasons why this would be impossible for their situation. It is too bad.

The spaces in between experiences can be just as important as the experiences themselves. I am just as busy as you are. But all of us need to get off the merry-go-round each and every day, or we risk losing the experience and ourselves as well. Plan some time today that you can just be. No activity, no telephone, no outside stimulation. Write it in your schedule if you have to. List it as an appointment with Mr. or Ms. Self. Make a habit of meeting this person every day. Spend a lot of time together on Shabbat.

If I am here, all are here; and if I am not here, who is here?
— TALMUD, SUKKAH 53A

Being present. Showing up. Sounds simple, but apparently it is not. As we can see from this day's quote (third–sixth century Babylonia), the problem is universal and timeless. We get easily distracted. We lose our focus. In spite of how wonderful our minds are, our attention span can be awfully short. To stay present—that is the challenge. For if I am not, then no one is.

Meditation is about focused energy. One focuses on a sound, a word or phrase, a thought, a visual symbol, a color, even one's breath. But the ultimate goal of meditation, I was taught in my practice of raja yoga, is to make one's *life* a meditation. Imagine if you brought that focus to everything you did. That is your meditation for today: How can I make my life a meditation?

Something is boring me—I think it's me.
— OSCAR WILDE

My little one says to me, "Abba, I'm bored. I have nothing to do." I answer, "How can you be bored? You know what happened today? The sun came up!" And then we talk.

The source of our boredom is not the lack of external stimuli. As a society we have more diversions, toys, activities, and games than people have had at any other time in the history of the world. And still boredom persists. The source of our boredom is ourselves, combined with the expectation that the world and others must keep us entertained. The world is not a boring place. Our minds and imaginations are rich enough resources to keep us interested, and interesting. It is we who fail to tap that resource from time to time.

If you are feeling bored, or that life is monotonous, ask yourself, "What is it that I am doing (or not doing) internally to create that feeling?" And as an antidote, think of all the miracles that are a daily part of our lives.

It is not necessary to have great things to do. I turn my little omelet in the pan for the love of God.
— BROTHER LAWRENCE

Again, the quality of our lives is not based on external experiences, as much as those experiences can add flavor to our existence. Rather, it is the consciousness we bring to each experience that determines who and what we are, that determines the contours and shapes of our lives. Jumping out of an airplane can become just as routine and boring as folding the laundry. However, when we live each moment, every action, consecrating them to God, then we lift up those acts even as they raise us up as well. This is the promise of every true religion.

In Judaism we say that there is no place, no act, devoid of God. Rather, God is wherever we let the Holy One in. As you go through your day, try to remember to invite God in to all your actions, big and small. Be aware of how this changes your experience of the day, and how you are changed by that experience.

How many are Your works, Adonai. The earth is full of Your creations.

— DAILY PRAYERBOOK

When was the last time you really looked at a flower? Or just sat back and watched a child at play? How often do you simply take a walk without a schedule or a specific destination? The world is an amazing place. We are incredible creatures. Life is a precious gift. And every moment, every object, has the potential to remind us of this truth. All we have to do is look and see, listen and hear, be present. There is no such thing as "been there, done that." We have never been here before. This moment has never existed in the history of the world and will never come again. You are a unique creation living a unique moment in time. That is all there is and that is everything.

Take a stone or some soil from a plant and place it in the palm of your hand. Sit with your eyes closed, saying and repeating to yourself, "I hold eternity in my hand." As you go through your day, try to take notice of all the "worlds" that surround you.

∼ ∼ ∼

meditations

AGING AND THE FRAGILITY OF LIFE

Do not cast me off in the time of my old age; when my strength fails me, do not forsake me.

— PSALM 71:9

With the changing of the clocks, the days appear even shorter. There is this recognition that sometimes makes us gasp—*our* days are also getting shorter, our lives are getting shorter; someday, maybe soon, we will no longer be. What will happen to us as we age? Will we lose our health? Will we stay sharp mentally? Will we survive the ones we love? Will we have enough to take care of our needs?

The psalmist reflects a universal, timeless concern. When we no longer have the strength of youth, will others (including God) see us as useless and unnecessary? Will our worth be measured only in terms of productivity? Will our gray hairs be the indicator of experience and wisdom, or a sign that we are "over the hill"?

I remember the first time a kid in the street called me "mister." I turned around to look for my dad. Then I suddenly realized, "He meant me! Oh no, have I become one of them?" How do you feel about getting older? What are your fears and your concerns?

Conditioned to operating as a machine for making and spending money, with all other relationships dependent upon its efficiency, the moment the machine is out of order and beyond repair, one begins to feel like a ghost without a sense of reality.
— RABBI ABRAHAM JOSHUA HESCHEL

Ask someone who they are, and after their name most will tell you their occupation. We have become so identified with our work that we tend to think that is who we are. No wonder so many people experience a crisis when it comes time for retirement. It is not merely the time they will have on their hands; it is a loss of identity. And it extends to the current debate on euthanasia and assisted suicide. When we are no longer "contributing" members of society, we regard our lives as essentially over.

But we are not what we do, at least not exclusively. We are, first and foremost, a *neshama*, a soul, a life force . . . breathed into us by God and one day returning to the Source of All Life. That is what makes us us, what makes us unique. And it can continue to grow and develop no matter how old or infirmed we may yet come to be.

Think of all the "things" you are, other than your occupation. Make an "I am _____" list.

The disappointment of manhood succeeds the delusion of youth.
— BENJAMIN DISRAELI

Coming to terms with all that we are not and will never be is part of the aging/growing old process. Living in cyclical time (in which every year is a microcosm of life itself), we have a yearly opportunity to confront this disappointment and evaluate what it means in terms of our identity and sense of self. And disappointment it is. The pain we feel is real. In part, it is because we have fallen short of our hopes, dreams, and expectations. But the other part stems from the fact that some of those hopes, dreams, and expectations are based on youthful delusions—self-delusions and the ones laid upon us by others. Some of the work of aging, then, part of what makes it an exhilarating time of life, is the sorting out of the basis for our disappointments. What is ours; what comes from others; what are the fantasies of youth? This is a time of great and painful honesty, of deep introspection, of a careful inventory of the inner workings of our hearts and minds. The clock is ticking away. We have nothing to fear.

What are your disappointments? What is their source?

To be old is a glorious thing when one has not unlearned what it means to begin.

— MARTIN BUBER

I have met, as I am sure we all have, old people who "do not seem old." I am not talking about physical appearance or a healthy vitality; these are either the gift of heredity or the skill of a surgeon's

knife. While I have nothing against people looking younger or maintaining their health, to equate these with youth is a prejudice against aging that we all need to overcome. To be old is not a negative. And when we say that someone "does not appear old" we have to make sure we have freed ourselves from all the pejorative connotations that old age has acquired in our time.

Life is about change. Nothing remains static or constant. To be able to start anew is the essence of real living. The true fountain of youth. Those who can combine the perspective of age with the willingness to begin again are the people who never seem to age.

How do you feel about beginnings? How can you make sure you never forget what it means to begin?

> *The righteous bloom like a date palm; they thrive like a cedar in Lebanon. Planted in the house of Adonai, they flourish in the courts of our God. In old age they still produce fruit. They are full of sap and freshness.*
>
> — PSALM 92:13–15

Years ago, I worked as an orderly in an old age home. I was trying to decide if I wanted to be a physician, and I thought that starting at the bottom would offer a good perspective from which to make my decision. Some of the people I encountered were bitter about being there, hateful of the family members who had placed them in the home. Others were cheerful, even grateful that they were being well taken care of. The head nurse who trained explained that old age merely brings out what is already there youth. Getting sent to an old age home does not embitter anyo

We are always becoming the person we are yet to be. If we w an old age filled with vitality and freshness, the time to start so those seeds is now. Planting them in the service of God is one to insure a bountiful harvest.

What seeds are you planting for your old age?

In middle age, you go to bed hoping you'll feel better in the morning. In old age, you go to bed hoping you'll have a morning.

— GROUCHO MARX

The night is a time of darkness, uncertainty, and fear. In Judaism, as in other religions, there is a prayer for the night, asking for God's protection, hoping for another day of life. (I have written one based on the traditional *Hashkivenu*. You can find it on page 23.) One of the follies of youth is our sense of immortality. We take risks with our lives; we assume life itself. The truth is, life is fragile. It is given one day at a time and can be taken away from us at any moment. We, or a loved one, need simply be standing at the wrong place at the wrong time for tragedy to strike and forever alter our lives. It has happened. It happens.

As we age, we become more and more aware of this reality. It is, in large measure, one of the rewards of old age—to appreciate with greater and greater depth the gift that is our lives.

If you have not already done so in the workout, thank God for this day. How will you use it? What will you add to yourself? To others?

～ ～ ～

meditations

DESPAIR

Futility of futilities, futility of futilities. All is futile.

— ECCLESIASTES 1:2

Each Jewish holiday and season has a biblical book associated with it. On Passover we read Song of Songs, with its celebration of spring and the sense of rebirth that falling in love brings. On

Shavuot it is the Book of Ruth, Purim's book is Esther, and on Sukkot it is *Kohelet*/Ecclesiastes. It is the somber reflection of an older or middle-aged man looking back at his life of accomplishments. And he begins by saying that everything is futile, that all our efforts don't amount to much.

In the middle of our year (i.e., life), even after a successful harvest (i.e., accomplishments), we are prone to despair. What does it all mean? What does it matter? All my strivings, all my gains—so what? What have I really accomplished? The answer most of us seem to feel, at least at some point in our lives, is "not much." And so, we might very well despair.

When and if you do, give voice to it. Don't try to hold it back. Read Psalm 6. Have a good cry. Share your depths with another (one who will not try to "solve" your feelings) or with God.

Never despair. But if you do, work on in despair.
                                               — EDMUND BURKE

It would be best if we never fell into despair. No matter how bleak things appear, we need to know that God is with us, that God will get us through. Yet, we do despair. We panic. We feel that we have come to the end of our line, that we are powerless to change our lives, that anything we might do will come to naught. We do despair. We hit rock bottom. It is often part of the aging process, part of coming to terms with our own mortality. Or it can just be part of our regular cycle of shifting energies and chemical/hormonal balance.

So when you despair, do not fight it or deny it; just keep on going. Keep "working" while you are going through it. Do what needs to be done. Use everything you have to get through your day. Despair does not need to be the end. Though it will not feel like it at the time, there will be a next day.

Imagine your despair as a tunnel. It can be as long and as dark as you want it to be. But no matter the length or the darkness, look to the end. And there, see the light that surrounds the exit, attempting to break in.

What soap is for the body, tears are for the soul.
— YIDDISH FOLK SAYING

As our bodies get dirty, so do our souls feel sadness. But neither of these situations have to be a permanent condition; there is a remedy. For dirt, there is soap. For despair, there are tears. Using soap does not mean we will never get dirty again; nor does crying mean we will rid ourselves of despair and sadness once and for all. But they help. They prevent too much buildup. And they remind us of the temporary condition of our affliction. For when we despair, the worst part of it is that we tend to think it will never end. Are there tears you are holding back right now? Why? Are you afraid that if you start crying, you will never stop? That the sadness will overwhelm you? Release your tears. Let them cleanse your soul.

Get really dirty and smelly. As you wash your body in the shower, imagine that the dirt and smells are your sadness. Watch them go down the drain.

You cannot prevent the birds of sorrow from flying over your head, but you can prevent them from building nests in your hair.
— CHINESE PROVERB

Sorrow and despair will come to each of our lives. That is reality. There is no life free of such moments. None. Religion, when understood properly, helps us, prepares us to experience and accept pain and sorrow as part of the all of life. It does not make it go away, nor does it anesthetize us to the feelings that accompany such moments. Rather, it gives us perspective and a sense of our place in the world of being. By doing these meditations, you are doing a truly religious act—living life fully, and with a sense of meaning and purpose.

There is a time for despair. Kohelet himself says it in words that were immortalized in song—"To everything there is a season . . ." There is a time to break down, and then a time to let it go, to make sure despair does not become a permanent feature in the landscape of our lives. That is what Jewish mourning customs—shivah (seven days), *shloshim* (thirty days), and *yahrzeit* (one-year anniversary)— are all about. They help us through the stages of our grief, to express it even while they confine our grieving. To remind us to let it go.

What sadness has nested in your life? Are you ready to chase the birds away? If not, why not? If you are, go out to your nearest park, wherever pigeons or birds gather. Sneak up quietly behind them and then in one quick motion, lift your arms out from your sides and into the air. And watch those birds fly.

All of us suffer, now as well as in ancient times, but not all are unhappy, for unhappiness is a reaction to suffering, not suffering itself.

— ALAN WATTS

We are always making choices, even when we think we are not. When hard times befall us, there is a tendency to blame others, to blame the situation, to blame our childhood, to blame everybody and everything but ourselves. This is not to say that it is all us. Of course, we are part of an environment and everything has an effect on everything else in our world. Others hurt us, our parents made mistakes or abused us, things happened beyond our control that brought great pain and suffering into our lives. All of this is part of the human condition. But in the end, there is still our response. And for that, we are the only ones responsible.

We may think that unhappiness is part of the experience of suffering, that they are one and the same. But they are not. Think of other possible reactions. Make a list. Ask someone you know who has suffered a great deal but does not seem to be unhappy how s/he does it.

Have you chosen unhappiness as your response to the suffering you are experiencing (or have experienced)? You are entitled to that choice. Say it. "I have chosen to be unhappy as a reaction to my suffering." Say each day that you are choosing unhappiness.

Sometimes I go about in pity for myself. And all the while a great wind is bearing me across the sky.

— OJIBWA

When despair hits us and bowls us over, it is sometimes all we can do to get through each day. That's okay. No one should expect any more. But even in such moments, when we are most likely to forget, it is important for us to remember that God is holding us, bearing us, helping us to get through. It is like that popular story of the footprints in the sand. When we see only one set of prints, it is because God is carrying us. So many have forgotten this basic truth in our time. So many, even those who say they "believe in God," have abstracted the Holy One into some kind of force within themselves. But Judaism asserts that God is a present reality concerned with each and every one of our lives—holding you, holding me.

Remember the trust fall? How we just had to let go and realize others would catch us? Do a trust fall with God. Lie down, or float on water, and imagine yourself falling through space. Before you hit bottom, feel yourself being caught and supported. These are the hands of God. Hands that will never, ever fail you.

❧ ❧ ❧

meditations
ACCEPTANCE / BALANCE / PERSPECTIVE

Most of us go through life not knowing what we want, but feeling darn sure this isn't it.

— ANONYMOUS

Never having enough stems from our feeling of never being enough. No matter what we accomplish, there always seems to be something we did not get to do. We even denigrate our successes, for after all, how good can they be if it is we who did them? I am not sure where or how this condition arises (we often blame our parents) but many of us suffer from it. Of this I have no doubt.

If it motivates us to do more, to try harder, to have high standards, then some good comes from "never being enough." But I am afraid that for most of us, this is a neurotic condition that prevents us from feeling real pleasure or contentment in our lives.

As we move toward the winter of our lives, we begin to let go of all those voices in our head that say "this isn't it." Time is running out. There will be nothing else. I must learn to accept and appreciate whatever it is that I have, whatever it is that I have become, whatever it is that I have or have not done. Can you practice affirming that? Say: "I accept that I have _____; I accept that I have accomplished _____; I accept that I am _____." Try it.

Do not covet your neighbor's wife. Do not desire your neighbor's house, his field, male or female servant, his ox or donkey, or anything that belongs to your neighbor.

— DEUTERONOMY 5:18

Seems like a simple enough formula. Do not want anything that belongs to someone else. Period. And I would guess this is one of the most—if not *the* most—violated commandments in the entire Torah. We are always wanting what someone else possesses. Despite the fact that we know it is not, the grass continues to look greener on the other side. Why is that? And why would the Torah command us to something that appears so impossible to fulfill?

There was once an antidrug commercial that voiced the thoughts of a young boy. Perhaps you heard it. The basic premise was that when he grew up, the boy was going to be a drug addict. He goes through a litany of the terrible things he would need to do as an addict—steal from his parents, live in the streets, etc. The irony is obvious. No one starts out with the intention to ruin his life; it just begins and grows from there. So our sages thought about our relationship with God. No one thinks, "I will distance myself from the Creator of All Life." But we begin to do so by coveting. For more than anything else, coveting is a denial of reality, of what is, and it drives a wedge between us and others, between us and God. The commandment not to covet reminds us to look to ourselves, to want what we are capable of achieving and acquiring, not what belongs to someone else.

What do you want that belongs to someone else? Do you really want it, or do you just think you do because someone else has it?

A person's feet are his guarantors. They take him wherever he is meant to be.

—TALMUD, SUKKAH 53A

I grew up hearing that I could be anything I wanted to be. Part of the American dream—third generation, grandson of immigrants. I am sure my parents thought this message was one that would build my self-esteem. Instead, it created a false sense of reality and a feeling of never really having achieved very much.

A far better message would have been, "You can be whatever your talents and abilities allow you to become." That is much more realistic, much more doable. And I hope that is what has, in fact, happened. We all have notions about who we are and what we are meant to be. Our feet can be our reality check. Wherever they are, so are you. It may not be where you thought you would be, but there you are, nonetheless.

Where have your feet taken you? Can you accept that this is where you are meant to be (at least for now)?

There is no person that does not have his hour, and no thing that does not have its place.

— PIRKE AVOT 4:3

This is as much a reminder to ourselves as it is a truth about others and the world around us. There is no person, no life without meaning, without purpose. Everyone has some appointed task or mission in life, without which the world would not be the same. If one has yet to discover it, no matter—s/he will. That is why every soul is precious. That is why we need everyone. Including that obnoxious person you wish would go away and leave you alone. Including you.

What is the hour and place for which you have been born into this world?

And if the way is too long for you to carry your tithe, turn it into money, hold the money tightly in your hand, and go to the place which Adonai your God will show you.

— DEUTERONOMY 14:24–5

Our sages taught that the reason the Torah tells us that the money should be in our hand is to remind us that it is we who ought to be in possession of our material goods, rather than allowing them to be in possession of us. Money is not the root of all evil. And poverty is not a virtue. There is nothing inherently wrong with being a wealthy person; it will not endanger one's chances to enter heaven. Judaism teaches that money is merely a means to an end. And that end, first and foremost, is to serve God and take care of God's creation, including oneself and one's family.

But so many of us have gotten out of balance when it comes to money. We live and work as its servants, rather than the other way around. Far from bringing us peace of mind and freedom to do what we want with our lives, money seems to entrap lots of people I know. They are working harder, spending less time with family and friends, enjoying it less. Even their vacations and their free time are frenetic. Money has taken possession of us.

Are your money and possessions working for you, or are you working for them? How do you know?

To everything there is a season, and a time to every purpose under heaven.

— ECCLESIASTES 3:1

Most people I counsel see the negative, hard times in life as something to get through en route to the good times that await them or that they remember from the past. My job, most often, is to get them to be willing to look at the negative moments as part of the pattern of existence, to look for their lessons and even their blessings, to look at why they have "chosen" those negatives— what they can teach them about themselves.

There is a season for everything. A time and a purpose. We may not know it while we are going through trials. We may even reject the idea as ludicrous. But all of our lives are an ebb and a flow, a balance. And the time comes, in our years, in our lives, when we must come to accept all that is, all that we are.

What part of you and your life have you yet to accept? Why is that? What are you rejecting as extraneous, as something that does not belong to you, as something you do not deserve?

WINTER

UNDERSTANDING

Use all your means to acquire understanding . . . for its reward is greater than silver or gold, more precious than rubies, and all the things one may desire cannot be compared to it.
— PROVERBS 3:13–15

We used to live in a society that valued things like wisdom and understanding, saw them as the basis for true happiness and peace. They were acquired slowly, through a lifetime of experience, and only by precious few individuals. Today, we tell our children to be happy by acquiring degrees, power, material wealth, and love. The former values are internal, and once acquired can never be taken away; the latter are external, based on others and on things over which we can have little control. We spend our lives pleasing others so that we can acquire all those things outside of us, and then drive ourselves crazy trying to hold on to them. But it rarely works. And we lose it all.

What do you value? What are you using your means to acquire?

Understanding is the reward of faith. Therefore, seek not to understand that you may believe; but believe that you may understand.
— ST. AUGUSTINE

Understanding is not some intellectual pursuit. Some people believe that if they take enough courses and acquire the right degrees, they will have understanding at the end. That is not the way it works. And the path of faith, the spiritual journey, while it has to be aided by our intellect to help us sort out the wheat from the chaff, is not the result of intellectual processes. In fact, without faith, without letting go of our self-dependence, without reliance on God, we will never come to any real understanding of the world or our place in it. When confronted with the Torah for the very first time, our people said, "*na'aseh v'nishmah/*We will do, and then we will understand." Understanding is the reward of faith. It comes from our willingness to go forward on this journey. It comes from our religious doing.

Are you waiting to understand before you fully commit yourself to this spiritual journey?

> *What is insight? It is the awareness that the external world is but a mirror. Whatever you see therein is but reflection of yourself.*
> — BA'AL SHEM TOV

Somewhere in modernity we got this notion that there is an objective reality out there, and that if we were good enough scientists/scholars, we could know and understand it. The Japanese film *Rashomon*, in which a single incident is shown from four different perspectives reminds us that all we have is our perception of things and that what we perceive is influenced by who we are. Scientists have confirmed this even on the subatomic level—even the path of the smallest of particles is influenced by the presence of an observer. We are inextricably a part of our surroundings, influenced by them, influencing what occurs in them. We are the sum total of our experiences. We see life as through a lens, shaped and colored by our personalities, our philosophies of life, our thoughts and feelings. There is no "out there" that is exactly the same for all of us. The world is but a mirror to our selves.

Write down five of your most cherished beliefs about the world, people, God, reality, etc. The things that you believe to be really true. Read them as a description of yourself. What do they say about you? You can ask a friend to do the same thing. Compare lists. What does his/her list say about your friend?

The heart sees better than the eye.

— LEO ROSTEN

There are many kinds of seeing. And all are important. All of them add something to our experience of life. Seeing with our eyes helps us to appreciate the grandeur and beauty of God's creation. It helps us to develop an aesthetic sensibility through which our surroundings add to our spirituality. But the internal seeing, the one we do with our hearts . . . this we must learn to do if we are to acquire understanding.

How do we "see" with our hearts? When we are not distracted by what a person looks like, when we feel the vibrations of a place before we look at its surroundings, when we intuit without analyzing, when we hear and don't just listen, when we are totally and fully present in each moment—then we see with our hearts. And often, this can be far better than the seeing we do with our eyes.

Practice seeing with your heart today. It may help if you close your eyes. At the end of the day, write down what you "saw."

To understand is to live with "what is," which does not mean to be contented with "what is." On the contrary.

— J. KRISHNAMURTI

I asked my nine-year-old son (during the middle of the summer) if he was looking forward to going back to school. I thought I was joking. He said, "Abba, if we look forward to something in the future, we may miss what there is for us to see and do in the present. You taught me that." Don't you just hate it when they listen! And then quote you!

The truth is that this moment, now, is all there is. The past is gone; all we have of it are our memories and the stories we tell. The future is not yet; all we have of it are our hopes and expectations. But the present is real. And understanding requires that we live with it and within it. Not like it, necessarily. Not even accept it as the final word. We are agents of change, and part of our task as human beings is to apply ourselves toward the ongoing task of perfecting the world. So we do not have to assume that what is will always be. But unless and until we see the world as it really is in this moment, unless we can live with it, then we will never acquire the understanding to do anything about it.

What is the reality of your life, right now? What would you like to change?

O God, Creator of humankind, I do not aspire to comprehend You or Your creation, nor to understand pain or suffering. I aspire only to relieve the pain and suffering of others, and trust in doing so, I may understand more clearly Your nature.

— ST. FRANCIS OF ASSISI

So you want to understand God? You want to know the secrets of the universe? You want to have a handle on the truth with a capital T? Then volunteer some time at the homeless shelter, serve on the soup line, take in a foster child, organize a clothing drive, help someone find a job. Unfortunately, the list is fairly endless, and seemingly growing longer these days. We often seek understanding in our study of abstractions. We think that seeking to understand is a task reserved for those who remove themselves from the everyday realities of the world and its people. Nothing could be further from the truth.

"You seek enlightenment?" the Zen master asked. "When you are hungry, eat; when you are sleepy, sleep." And I would add, help others to do the same.

See if you can go out and relieve someone else's pain and suffering today. Afterward, ask yourself this question: "What understanding of God and the universe did I acquire through my action?" (This is a good one to repeat. Even if you do not acquire any understanding, you will be making the world a better place in which to live for yourself and others.)

～ ～ ～

m e d i t a t i o n s
WISDOM

If you have wisdom, then what do you lack? If you lack wisdom, then what do you have?

— TALMUD, NEDARIM 41A

We live in a time and place that does not really value wisdom. We value power, money, youth and good looks, physical prowess. Our heroes are actors, rock stars, and athletes. We may still pay lip service to wisdom, but in truth we will admire someone who is clever or smart, someone who can solve problems or be creative, but not someone who is really wise.

Our quote comes from an age in which wisdom was the most important value. If one had wisdom, one had everything, or at least everything that mattered. Wisdom comes from age, from experience, from a deeper kind of knowing. Wisdom requires a rich spiritual reservoir, an internal calm, acceptance, and compassion. One who is wise relates easily and comfortably with others and the world, sees to the core of the matter, looks into our souls. Wisdom cannot be purchased or learned; rather, it is acquired or gifted after a lifetime of seeking.

Where is your wisdom? In what area of life are you wise (or seeking to be)? Fill in the blank: I am wise when I _____.

The ways of a simpleton seem proper to him, but the one who accepts counsel is wise.

— PROVERBS 12:15

Somehow people, especially men, have gotten this notion that to accept help is a sign of weakness and that to ask the advice of another is a mark of imperfection. So we go about our lives pretending we know it all, or that we can figure it out on our own. I call it the "independence mythos" with which we are destroying ourselves and the world around us.

I attended an open school night in which one of my son's teachers was explaining that he took off points from a student's class grade if s/he was missing a pencil, paper, or some other item. I asked if students were given the opportunity to borrow from classmates so long as they did not disrupt the class. The teacher responded, "Oh, no. I want them to learn to be self-reliant." I responded that knowing how and whom to ask for help were essential life skills that I hoped would be equally valued. And that our ability to receive help from others is the mark of true wisdom. I don't think he got it.

What are the things you would like to know with which you need some help or advice?

Accustom your tongue to say, "I do not know."

— TALMUD, BERACHOT 4A

This is the flip side of learning to ask for help and advice. It is also the beginning of wisdom. We cannot know it all. The world is too vast, and growing each day. To become an expert in any one field takes a lifetime, and the amount of material one must master in order to do so is enormous. Though the information superhighway may be at our fingertips, to travel all the lanes is an impossibility. We just have to get used to saying, "I don't know."

The Talmud understood this reality more than a thousand years ago. It begins on page *bet,* or two, in order to teach us that wisdom is like an ocean, with no real beginning and no real end. We just need to jump in at any time or place and start swimming.

Do you have a hard time saying, "I don't know"? Why is that?

Rabbi Elazar ben Azarya used to say: When our wisdom exceeds our deeds, to what can we be compared? To a tree with many branches but few roots; a wind comes along and uproots the tree . . . But when our deeds exceed our wisdom, to what can we be compared? To a tree with many roots and few branches. Though all the winds of the world would come and blow against it, they would be unable to uproot the tree.

— PIRKE AVOT 3:22

Appearances can be deceiving. And wisdom that detaches us from the rest of the world is not really wisdom at all. Those who set about their lives acquiring that kind of wisdom are like the trees with few roots. Though they might look substantial to the undiscerning eye, though they may appear to be quite beautiful, bearing fruit and providing shade, in truth they will be unable to weather the first storm. Our wisdom ought to lead us into the world of action, of doing, especially for others. This is the strongest kind of tree, though it might not look like much from the outside. Nothing can shake it.

Has your quest for wisdom exceeded your deeds? How will you go about changing the balance?

Nothing being more important than anything else, a man of knowledge chooses any act, and acts as if it matters to him.
— DON JUAN (CARLOS CASTANEDA)

Many of us are frozen because we cannot decide what is most important. We search for truly "significant" things to do, activities worthy of our time and efforts, our skills and expertise, and meanwhile the world passes us by. In the monasteries of old, a novice would spend years washing the floors or doing some other equally mundane task. He would keep the assignment until he recognized the holiness intrinsic in what he was doing. In the same spirit, rabbis were enjoined to be householders and to have a "real job" beyond their rabbinic duties. Every task is necessary. Every positive act helps to bring about God's dominion on earth. Nothing is more important than anything else.

I have had this experience on more than one occasion: Everyone is helping carry chairs or engaging in some other form of schlepping. Suddenly I hear someone say, "Let me do that for you, Rabbi." I know the person means well by his or her attention, but the assumption that manual labor is beneath my so-called station in life misses the point. It is not the act that is the essential thing. It is simply how we carry it out.

What is it that you can/will do today? Will you act "as if" all of it matters?

Teach us, O God, to number our days, that we may acquire a heart of wisdom.
— PSALM 90:12

Each day is a gift. Recognizing that, counting your days (but not counting *on* them), is at the core of a wise and discerning heart. It is a heart that loves and appreciates life. It is a wisdom that values and makes the most of each day. That does not (necessarily) mean living at a frenetic pace, doing as much as we possibly can, squeezing into each day an endless stream of activities that keep us busy. Nor does it mean that life should be equated with the number of days allotted us—"the more the better." Rather, it means putting all of ourselves into everything we do. That is a heart of wisdom.

How do you number your days?

~ ~ ~

meditations
DEATH AND AFTERLIFE

If some messenger were to come to us with the offer that death should be overthrown, but with the one inseparable condition that birth should also cease; if the existing generation were given the chance to live forever, but on the clear understanding that never again would there be a new child, or a youth, or first love, never again new persons with new hopes, new ideas, new achievements; ourselves for always and never any others—could the answer be in doubt?

— GATES OF REPENTANCE, RABBI CHAIM STERN

After a death, I will ask the adult children how their surviving parent is. "Great . . . the doctor gave her/him something" is often the reply. After fifty or more years of marriage, we think, it is great that someone is so anesthetized that s/he does not feel anything. What is wrong with that picture?

We live in a death-denying culture. We are afraid to face the reality of death, so we hire others to take care of our dead and to make them look "lifelike." We shorten our time of mourning, rushing to get back to the office and our regular routines. And now we seem poised to pass laws that will legalize euthanasia, just so we do not have to deal with the death process. But death is not to be feared and cannot be denied. It is the ticket price of admission into this thing we call life. As we move toward the winter solstice and the shortest day of the year, we need to face the fact that the days of our lives are also growing shorter. Each day lived is another day closer to our death.

What bothers you about that last statement? What frightens you about death?

All my life has been given me merely that I might learn to die.
— RABBI SIMCHA BUNAM

Why do we have to "learn to die"? Isn't it enough that we will? It is because how we die is a measure of how we lived. It reveals our beliefs about the sanctity of life; about what we value and what is precious; about our relationships with those we have loved and who have loved us; about the worth of a human being; about the limits of the human body and the immortality of the soul; about our willingness to accept and deal with pain; about our faith in God. Accepting death and learning to die—these are two of our greatest spiritual challenges, universal challenges that none can escape. And that is why all cultures, all peoples throughout the history of the world have created their stories, their rituals and traditions that help them deal with the reality and inevitability of death. What we call "religion" is merely the accepted traditions of any one group. What is your life teaching you about how to die?

What profit is there in my blood when I go down into the pit?
Can dust praise You? Can it speak of Your truth?
— PSALM 30:10

Judaism is a life-affirming tradition. We love life. We toast, "*L'chaim!*/To life!" We understand life as a gift from God, given one day at a time. To spurn this gift would be an insult to the One who gave it. While other traditions see our time on earth as an unfortunate prelude to a more perfect, eternal existence beyond the body's death, Judaism continues to hold all life as precious. While we fully understand and accept the body's impermanence, while we recognize the eternalness of the soul, we still see life as the best time to act on our faith, to demonstrate our love of God and our loyalty to the covenant. And so even when life is unkind to us, even when we are in pain and in need of relief, still we cling to the hope of yet another hour, another day. We do nothing to hasten death. It is only by being alive that we can serve Adonai and do the Eternal's commandments.

What is most precious to you about being alive?

The meaning of life is that it stops.

— FRANZ KAFKA

It hurts to acknowledge the truth of this statement. But true it is. Death gives life its meaning because it makes it finite. The fact that we have it for a little while, without ever really knowing for just how long, is the best goad we have to make the most of it. Would that it could be different. Would that we were different. But we are not. And we know that because it stops, because it will be taken away from us, life has meaning, and purpose, and value. Every death we experience, every funeral we attend reminds of this fact. In this sense, death is not so much a punishment, as a reminder to live and love, to fill each day and give it our best. To fill it with meaning.

What are you doing that gives your life meaning?

Death is merely moving from one home to another.

— KOTZKER REBBE

I think the question I am asked more than any other is, "Rabbi, Jews don't believe in the afterlife, do we?" And to everyone's surprise, the answer is that while we have no dogma as to exactly what form the afterlife takes, Judaism has always affirmed that the body's death is not the end of the individual. While we are free to speculate about such things as heaven and hell, reward and punishment, the underworld, reincarnation, etc.—all of which have had exemplary Jewish proponents—Judaism insists that the life force we call *neshama*/soul continues beyond our physical existence here on earth. If our soul is energy, as I think it is, and if physicists are correct in telling us that energy cannot be created or destroyed, only changed in form, then after we die, the energy that was our soul/life force must continue to exist in some other form.

I was at a friend's country home when he pointed out a rather large beetle on a tree. As he brought me closer, he told me that it wasn't really a beetle, just its shell. There was a hole in the top of it. Apparently, this type of beetle eats its way out of the shell when it is no longer useful and then flies away to exist in another form. I said to him, "That is exactly what happens to us, only we call it death."

Take a deep breath. Now exhale. The words for soul and breath come from the same Hebrew root. *Neshama*=soul; *linshome*=to breathe. Do you hear the connection? "N," "Sh," "M"? Take another breath. Feel your life force, your breath, your soul. Now in. Now out. (NOTE: This is a good exercise to include in your workout, especially as you pray the blessing for the soul.)

Not to mourn is impossible, because the blow has fallen. But to mourn overmuch is also impossible, because we do not impose on the community a hardship which the majority cannot endure.
— TALMUD, BABA BATRA 60B

In my work as a congregational rabbi, I have buried lots of people. I have sat vigil with families and watched and prayed as a loved one clung to life. I have been there at the moment of passing, when the body could no longer hold out and we had to let go. And this I will tell you: It does not matter if the person has lived a long and productive life, or if it is someone with lots more to do and give—death is always sad. Funerals and mourning are times to cry, and holler, and beat our breasts. We have lost something that was part of us, and it hurts.

I understand that some traditions celebrate death. They reckon that their loved one has gone to a better place, and so they are happy for him/her. There are other traditions that put on the black clothes after their loss and never remove them. Neither of these are our way. We designate times, each successive one decreasing in severity—seven days, then thirty days, then one year—as appropriate periods to deal with our loss. We remember our beloved each year at the anniversary of their deaths (*yahrzeit*) and at *yizkor* (special worship services). And, of course, the heart has its own rhythm and its own way that cannot be prescribed. But to ask more than that would be to deny life itself and thus negate the very reason for our mourning. If life is precious, then we must go on living it. We mourn because a life has been lost. To spend our lives mourning would be to lose two lives.

What losses have you experienced? Did you allow yourself to mourn them? Are you still mourning them?

Note: The severity is not just emotional. It covers our activities as well, restricted in the first 7 days, then relaxing as time goes on.

CHANUKAH

❧

Like all Jewish holidays, Chanukah works on two levels. On the one hand it is the celebration of a military victory over the Syrian Greeks and the Hellenizing Jews who had turned the ancient Temple into a pagan shrine. It is also a winter solstice festival, taking place on or around the shortest days of the year. In the ancient world, as the days got shorter and shorter, the people must have believed that the sun could disappear altogether. And so, many cultures created rituals at the time of the winter solstice to reassure themselves of the light's return. This, too, is Chanukah. On the personal level, Chanukah represents our own death and hope for the rebirth of the soul.

❧   ❧   ❧

meditations
HOPE

Hope is an orientation of the spirit, an orientation of the heart. It is not only the conviction that something will turn out well, but the certainty that something makes sense, regardless of how it turns out.

— VÁCLAV HAVEL

For many of us, hope sounds like a cop-out. It may conjure up images of defenseless Jews praying for some messiah to save them, hoping for a miracle, powerless to protect themselves or their loved ones. But hope is not a relinquishing of personal responsibility. Rather, it is the conviction that our lives make sense, that they have meaning. Wouldn't it be great to say that with conviction? "Our lives make sense. They have meaning. We are not just arbitrary specks floating in the universe for an insignificant amount of time." Hope reminds us of that meaning. It is a sustaining belief even when there is no evidence to support it. It is spiritual medicine against the devaluation of human life, which has plagued us in modernity, turning us and our lives into a series of numbers and statistics and production quotas.

At this time of year, in the winter of our lives, when the days are at their shortest and the light has almost been extinguished, we must rely on our hope to get us through. The light will return. Spring will follow winter. Our lives make sense. They have ultimate meaning.

What is it that seems to make no sense in your life right now? Can you say, "Even though I do not see it at this time, _____ will somehow fit into the pattern that is my life"? Can you say that?

No matter how defeated we feel by the earthly events that swirl around us, we must remember that we have a spiritual identity that cannot be diminished or modified by external circumstances . . . The Talmud reminds us that the conscious exercise of hope is a gift we are obliged not to forsake. Faith in our enduring identity with God is the ladder of hope within each of our grasps.

— WRESTLING WITH ANGELS, NAOMI ROSENBLATT

We are all defeated from time to time. None of us can escape it. We fail. The world and circumstances knock us down. Others beat us. Sometimes, we even dig a hole for ourselves. Yet, as Jacob discovered in his dream, there are ladders all around, stretching from God to us, if only we would become aware of them. Hope is such a ladder. Knowing that we are one with God, that our essential identity is a spiritual one that transcends time and space, can help get us through.

There is the joke about a guy who is drowning in the ocean. Boats come by; helicopters fly overhead; submarines come up from the depths, all trying to save him. He refuses their help, insisting that he trusts only in God, and that God will save him. Finally, he can hold out no longer, and he drowns. Angrily, his soul confronts the Holy One in heaven for forsaking him. God replies, "I sent you a boat, I sent you a helicopter . . ." God is doing the same for each of us whenever we are drowning. All we have to do is reach out and grab the lifeline.

Do you feel all alone, abandoned by God? Imagine a ladder, stretching down from the heavens. Image yourself grabbing on to it and pulling yourself up. Feel the hand of God helping you the rest of the way.

> *Things may turn out successfully or not, happily or otherwise. Since there is at least as much chance of a favorable as an unfavorable outcome, why worry about the negative when you can enjoy anticipating the positive?*
>
> — MOSES MAIMONIDES

Talk about the power of positive thinking. Almost a thousand years ago Maimonides taught us that, at least in part, good health was dependent on thinking positive thoughts. To him, it was logical to do so. After all, we have a fifty-fifty chance that things will work out in our favor, so we might as well enjoy it, right? In our time, though it may seem crazy, positive imagery does seem to have a good effect on those who are suffering and in pain. I have no idea how that works; I am not even sure I want to know. But I have witnessed it on many occasions. For some of us, it may require that we go against our natural inclinations. Despite what we might want to think about ourselves, anxiety and negativity seem to dominate our consciousness whenever the outcome is uncertain. For others, it will require blocking out those negative thoughts that just seem to creep up on us no matter what we try to do. And it is doable. Imagine your future as a road stretching into the landscape. Picture some type of barrier or gate on that road. Personify each thought you have. Make each one ask permission at the barrier to continue traveling on the road. Negative travelers, no matter how convincing they try to be, must always be refused passage.

~ ~ ~

meditations

DARKNESS AND LIGHT

The School of Hillel says, "On the first day of Chanukah one candle shall be lit. Each subsequent night, one candle is added, so that on the eighth night there are eight lights."
— TALMUD, SHABBAT 21B

Winter solstice. The shortest day of the year is upon us. Just as it appears that the darkness will overwhelm us, engulf us, just as it appears that our lives are over, we are commanded to light lights. It begins with a single flame, and each night another is added. By the end we have a full menorah, eight candles, lighting our homes and lightening our hearts.

As you light your Chanukah menorah, think of all the others throughout the world who are doing the same. Imagine the world, then, encircled in light. This is our response to the darkness. To light a single flame. By itself, not very much, but when joined with others, it can light the way for humankind.

Think of all those throughout time who were denied the right to light this flame. Invite their spirits to join you each night of the festival.

It is only by recognizing the season of darkness that we know it is time to light the candles, to sow a seed of light that can sprout and spring forth later in the year.

— ARTHUR WASKOW

We do not curse the darkness. It, too, is our teacher, part of the pattern of the universe. Without it, we would not know when it is time to light our flames; without it, we would be unable to recognize the very light itself. Each of us has experienced darkness in our own lives. Some are sitting in the dark even as they read these words. We do not need to invite the darkness; it will arrive of its own accord. But we need not deny it, either. And we need not be too hasty in chasing it away. That we will do, one candle at a time. And the light will spring forth, later in the year, later in our lives. That, too, is part of the universe's pattern.

Think about the darkness in your life. What has it come to teach you? Can you thank God for sending you this darkness?

And we must extinguish the candle, put out the light and relight it. Forever must quench, forever relight the flame.

— T. S. ELIOT

We bring on the darkness. That is part of our human condition. And none can avoid it. But it does not have to remain that way. We have the power to transcend every darkness, to relight the extinguished flame. It is not always so easy. At times the effort seems hardly worth it. Nevertheless, we have to try. Our souls are very much like that: They, too, go out and then are relit. It is a pattern that goes on forever, reminding us that our souls can never be fully extinguished. The light goes out and then is relit. Forever.

Where is there darkness in your life, your world, your relationships? Where do you need to light some light? Try dedicating each
night of Chanukah to a different need. Say (either to yourself or out
loud), "I light these candles to cast light onto _____."

*On this night of dedication, we kindle our flame. May this light
shine with hope for the freedom of all people.*
— RABBI ELYSE FRISHMAN

The light that we cannot let go out is the light of Judaism, which
says that freedom and dignity are the birthrights of each and every
human being. Part of our mission, part of our task, has got to
include efforts to cast this light throughout the world. As we look
around us—and we do not have to look very far—we see that this
is not yet the condition of every person on this planet. We live in a
time of great prosperity, but the reality of millions is homelessness,
hunger, and even starvation. The concept of democracy was born
over two hundred years ago, and still assassination, torture, and
imprisonment stifle free speech and assembly. Violence, crime, war,
terrorism, discrimination based on gender, race, or sexual orientation, denial of God, abuse of children and spouses—our world is
beset by problems that hinder our full human potential, that
prevent us from becoming the person we were meant to be. We
must cast a light on this darkness that threatens our world and its
inhabitants.

What are you doing to keep the light of freedom and human
dignity burning?

*The light of a candle is useful when it precedes you; it is useless
when it trails behind.*
— BAHYA BEN ASHER

Sometimes we seem to be working as hard as we can, doing as much as possible, and still getting nowhere. We take a step forward only to take two back; our wheels keep spinning, but we are not moving anywhere. Problems beset us. Our issues feel overwhelming. And nothing is happening. Perhaps our candle is behind us.

No one intentionally puts the candle there; we all know that it will do us no good. But how many times does it seem to be there anyway? Placing the candle in front involves taking a risk. It means we can see, but we can also be seen. It means being vulnerable. And it also means moving ahead, leaving familiar ground, and that can be threatening, even scary. When we find the candle behind us, we have to ask ourselves, "Who put it there and why?"

Where is your candle right now? Is it lighting up your path or did you stick it someplace where it will do you no good?

Rejoice not, my enemy. For when I fall, I will rise. When I sit in darkness, God will be my light.

— MICAH 7:8

The ultimate message of Chanukah is that no matter how long and black the night appears to be, the darkness will not win. The light will return. It is inevitable. And we cannot give up. All of us have sat in darkness. It was a darkness that threatened to overwhelm us, to defeat us, to keep us bound forever. But you are still here, reading these words, looking for a way out. Though you may not know it or feel it, God is your light. God has been your light all along. And God will be your light wherever you go. For the Eternal One can do no other. God is always there, lighting your path through life.

Ask God to be your light. Go ahead. Ask.

~ ~ ~

meditations
MIRACLES

Days pass and the years vanish, and we walk sightless among miracles.

— GATES OF PRAYER, RABBI CHAIM STERN

When we think of miracles, biblical images of seas parting, one day's oil lasting for eight nights, or Joshua making the sun stand still all come to mind. And since none of us have ever witnessed anything like that, we dismiss the notion of miracles as something made up in a distant past to appease the primitive mind, believed today only by the gullible and the naive. But what if we have it all wrong? What if miracles are occurring all around us and we are simply blind to them? What if we're looking for the wrong thing? A flower blooms . . . a toddler begins to speak . . . we arrive safely at our work destination this morning. Are these not also miracles? Who says that a miracle can only be an inexplicable event? What if that is but one type of miracle? What if miracles are like those 3-D movies where if you don't have the right "glasses," you don't see the special effects in quite the same way?

The prayer from which today's quote is taken goes on to say, "Lord fill our eyes with seeing and our minds with knowing." Ask God to help you see and know in this way. Perhaps you may just witness a miracle or two.

The world will never starve for want of wonders; but only for want of wonder.

— G. K. CHESTERTON

In the preliminary blessings of the morning worship service, there is a list of blessings called *nissim b'chol yom,* which can be translated as "daily miracles." Once, these blessings were said at home, upon awakening, corresponding to every action that got one from sleeping to his or her first steps out of bed. Thank you, God, for making the rooster crow . . . thank you, God, for opening my eyes . . . thank you, God, for giving me the capacity to stretch my arms . . . for sitting upright . . . for this robe . . . You get the picture. Today I suppose we could substitute "alarm clock" for "rooster," end with a blessing for coffeemakers, and the list would pretty much be the same.* [*My translation of these blessings can be found in the Appendix. They can be added to your workout each day.] One of the great spiritual problems that confronts us as people is taking things for granted. It is a poison that kills both relationships and the individual soul. I call this list of blessings the Jewish antidote to taking things for granted. It asks us to look at every little thing we do, from the moment we wake up in the morning, as a miracle. A miracle! Not an ordinary event unworthy of our attention, but a miracle.

Though it may slow you down a bit today, start to reprocess your brain to think of any and all of the things you habitually do as miracles. Driving in the car pool . . . working on your computer . . . reading this book. Don't take any of them for granted.

A miracle is our capacity to see the common in an uncommon way.

— NOAH BEN SHEA

What is it that God saw in Moses that made him the right person for the task of leading the children of Israel out of Egyptian slavery? The answer our rabbis give is that Moses stopped to take a look at the burning bush. When God saw that Moses was willing to look at the world in that way, the Holy One realized that this was no ordinary man. And so Moses was chosen.

It matters little whether or not this story is historical reality or total fiction. Moses was alone at the time and so we will never know for sure what happened that day in the desert. But our people tell this story primarily for what it teaches us about Moses and, by extension, what it holds out for each of us. What if instead of searching for the unusual, we spent our energy taking a new look at all the ordinary, everyday occurrences in our lives? And what if instead of taking them for granted, we began to see that there really is nothing ordinary about them? Each day we perform a myriad of tasks, have dozens of encounters, look out at others and our world. If we could but stop and consider each of these as something new, something that has never existed before (which is the truth), would it not be a miracle? Our tradition teaches us that a miracle has more to do with what is going on inside of us than what is happening in the world around us. The miracle is the way we see.

Today, choose three habitual activities that you engage in each day. As you are doing them, pretend this is the first time you have ever done so, or pretend that you are someone else watching yourself do them. What do you see?

The mitzvah of Chanukah is to display the menorah prominently where it can be see by all passersby, in order to publicize the great miracle.

— SHULCHAN ARUCH

Remember the movie *The Wizard of Oz*? Remember the Cowardly Lion's repeating to himself with his eyes closed, "I do believe . . . I do believe . . ."? The menorah in our window, besides its obvious proclaiming of Jewish identity, is a way of saying, "I do believe in miracles." Whether it is the miracle of a single cruse of oil lasting eight nights; the miracle of a small band of warriors defeating the mighty Syrian army; the miracle of a persecuted people surviving and preserving a way of life; or the miracle of the seasons and the sun's certain return, it does not matter. The menorah says, "I do believe." And what a miracle it is, that after all our trials there are still Jews in the world willing and able to place a menorah in the window of their home and declare this belief. A miracle indeed.

What are the miracles of your life? Which are you ready to publicly proclaim?

A miracle does not prove what is impossible; rather, it is an affirmation of what is possible.
— MOSES MAIMONIDES (RAMBAM)

Modernity taught us to be rational and critical. It asked us to use our left-brain function to analyze, to scientifically experiment, to not fall prey to superstition, convention, or habit. To the extent that it provided a balance to the excesses of the past, it was a healthy corrective. But being rational is not the same as being cynical or pessimistic. It does not mean we must debunk anything that seems inexplicable. Another way of thinking about miracles is to reflect on what they say about us, not just the world and our way of looking at it. Are we still able to dream? To imagine? To hope? Or have we become so boxed in by our rationality that the world is simply a place in which everything is either predictable or beyond our consideration? Believing in miracles nurtures that place inside of us in which we can affirm that anything is possible, and that God is not limited by the scope of our imagination.

What have you given up on as no longer possible? What does that say about you?

Miracles, no matter how inexplicable or unbelievable, are real and can occur without regard to the natural order of things.
— NICHOLAS SPARKS

Not so long ago, I visited the archaeological site of Bethsaida, mentioned prominently in the New Testament as the place where Jesus walked on water. The problem in locating this ancient village was that the site they found that fit the description was not near any water. Yet there were fishing nets, anchors, and other signs of a seaside town. And then geologists solved the problem. The waters of the Sea of Galilee, never very deep on this shore, receded over the centuries and dried up. As the city got to be farther and farther away from the water, it was eventually abandoned. But in its heyday, in the summer months, one could walk on the rocks in the very shallow water and appear to be walking on water.

As moderns, we were trained to believe that every so-called miracle can be explained away, if only we had all the facts. But the reality of our lives tells us this is not the case. There are occurrences in life that are really and truly miracles—people being cured of cancer and other diseases, surviving accidents and tragedies, being reunited with long-lost family members. I am sure you can think of others. Not everything acts according to the laws of nature. Not everything is predictable. Miracles can and do happen.

Do you still believe in miracles? Can you open yourself up to their possibility? What is stopping you? Ask God's help in letting it go.

meditations

REDEDICATION

At the very season and on the very day that the altar had been profaned, it was rededicated with songs and harps and lutes and cymbals. All the people prostrated themselves, worshiping and praising Heaven who had prospered them.

—I MACCABEES 4:4–5

When the Maccabees came to the ancient Temple in Jerusalem, they found that the purpose for which it had been created—worship of God—had been perverted and misappropriated. Refusing to be defeated, they recycled all of its holy vessels and began anew.

In the course of a year, or the course of our lives, each of us loses our way, fails to make use of our gifts, our talents, our promise. Each of us faces monumental difficulties, or powers greater than ourselves that wish us to give up the struggle. To rededicate ourselves is to make movement in the face of whatever it is that comes to tell us that we cannot, that we are doomed, that our efforts will go unrewarded. To rededicate is to begin again.

At this time of the year, in the dead of winter, we begin the process of getting ready for spring. We take all that is lying dormant, everything whose potential remains unrealized, and with song and celebration consecrate it for its fulfillment.

What lies dormant in you? What plan remains unrealized, what ability under-utilized? Take time this week to celebrate it and dedicate yourself anew to the fulfillment of God's purpose.

Spiritual growth is rarely continuous, but is rather marked by pauses and plateaus. It is like going uphill in a wagon—there is upward progress only so long as there is active movement. But when the wagon comes to a stop, it will slip and roll back down.
— RABBI MICHEL OF ZLOTCHOW

Winter (and it could be the actual season of winter or simply "the winter of our lives") is a time of pause and plateau. A time of hibernation. A time to hunker down and gather our strength for the spring that will follow. It is rarely a time of forward progress. In winter, we are like that wagon that has stopped on the hill—we find ourselves having stopped in our spiritual growth; perhaps we have even slipped back a little. If we were a wagon, blocks behind the wheels might help prevent any backward movement. Our commitment to rededication does the same. It tells us that while this pause is normal, even necessary at times, a spring will follow and we will move on again.

Imagine your life as that wagon, poised on the hill. What will you do to get going again?

> *If our lives have become shallow, deepen them;*
> *If our principles have become shabby, repair them;*
> *If our ideals have become tarnished, restore them.*
> — LIKRAT SHABBAT, RABBI SIDNEY GREENBERG
> AND RABBI JONATHAN D. LEVINE

A physician friend of mine was telling me once that he had stopped going to medical conventions. When I asked him why, he proceeded to tell me that the only thing his colleagues were interested in talking about was the business of running a medical practice. "Whatever happened to all our idealism about medicine?" he asked. I have a feeling he would have had the same complaint had he been something other than a doctor. At times, it is not all that different in a rabbinic conference. Whatever happened, indeed, to our ideals and principles? Do we all wind up being practitioners, concerned above everything else with paying the bills, not getting sued, sending the kids to a decent college, and having enough for retirement? I sure hope not.

Our youth was a time of great idealism. Sure, some of it was naïveté, but certainly not all of it. We need to pray for God's help in making certain we do not become cynical, callous, or sarcastic. We need to ask God to help restore in us the belief that everything is possible, if we but believe and will it and work for it to be so. Our lives need to be driven, not by the bottom line, not by what is cheap or popular, but by the values that got us here in the first place. And this is the time of the year for it. What are the ideals, values, and principles by which you (wish to) live your life?

In this New Year, may the roof of your house not fall in and the people who live in it not fall out. And if they do, may they make up again.

— Swedish proverb

When I ask people what the most important thing in their lives is, they invariably answer, "My relationships with spouse, children, family, and friends." Yet when we take a close look at their lives, it becomes perfectly clear that relationship-building occupies the least amount of time in their actual calendar. I believe them when they say how important these relationships are, but somehow we think that relationships are going to happen without much effort on our parts, that they are going to miraculously take care of themselves. But it does not happen that way. Relationships have to be worked on. They have to become a priority. And when there has been a falling-out or a falling away, and it feels as if the roof has fallen in on our heads, we must rededicate ourselves to what is best in those relationships, so that they may continue to be a positive element in our lives.

What relationships in your life have "fallen out of your house"? What steps are you willing to take to bring them back in?

Turn us, Adonai, and we will return to You. Renew our days as in days gone by.

— Prayer upon returning the Torah to the ark

Once, we were there; at one with God. But in the course of a year, in the course of a lifetime, we lose our way, we get a little lost. We go to places where we really do not want to be. We get stuck in positions we have taken and now feel the need to defend. Often we have tried to stay on course, but in truth, we lost hope, lost sight of the real goal. And now, in the winter of our days, we wish to return but we recognize the need for God's help in doing so. We cannot do this work alone. We have gone as far as we can on our own. Probably our friends and family have been our support in getting us this far. But now it is up to God. The ark is opened for the Torah's return. Plaintively we call out, we cry in our hearts, "Turn us, Adonai, turn us . . . we cannot get there on our own . . . we know that now . . . we have been stubborn thinking we did not need you . . . but now we know . . . turn us around and we will return to you . . . we want it to be as it once was between us . . . renew us . . . renew our days." And then the ark is closed and the Torah is put away. It is a window of opportunity.

Imagine the curtains of the ark are pulled back right now. Today, you can ask God to renew your life. Today. What is stopping you?

Unless God builds the house, its builders labor in vain.
— PSALM 127:1 (SAID WHEN A MEZUZAH IS PUT UP IN A NEW HOME)

One of the tragedies of the modern era for us as Jews is that we have forgotten that our homes are supposed to be a *mikdash m'at,* a small sanctuary dedicated to the sanctification of day-to-day, so-called mundane acts. It is the home, not the synagogue, that is the center of Jewish life. Yet many of us live as if we "do Jewish" primarily at Temple, and only secondarily at home. Part of the reason for this is that we have forgotten (or never knew) what to do. We feel incompetent or even illiterate as Jews, and so we avoid being embarrassed by attempting to say and do things for which we have little facility. After all, we are expert in so many things. Why do that which will only make us feel bad and ashamed?

But another part of the reason is that we have bifurcated our lives into the Jewish/religious versus the secular. Temple is for the former; home/work/play are for the latter. Judaism knows no such separation. For us, every moment has the potential to be sanctified, blessed by us and blessed by God.

When we put a mezuzah on the doorpost of our home, we are saying that this will be a place that we dedicate to God's service. Why not rededicate your home to that purpose this year? What will you say? What will you want to do in a home dedicated to God? What will you try to avoid?

～　　～　　～

meditations
Rebirth/Self-Renewal

All beginnings require that we unlock new doors.
— Rabbi Nachman of Bratzlav

For those of us who grew up or live in wintry climates, it is strange to be thinking of this time as a moment of rebirth and self-renewal. Outside, all is frozen underneath a blanket of snow. It feels more like a time of hibernation, of going inside, literally and spiritually. But the truth is, the shortest day of the year has passed. By a couple of minutes each day, we are adding light, moving inexorably toward spring. All things contain their opposite. Locked away, inside the depths of winter and darkness, are the seeds of rebirth and renewal. At the very beginning of this change, then, it is appropriate for us to pause and take notice, preparing ourselves for the new life that is our certain promise.

Which doors remain locked in your life? Will this be the year you choose to unlock them? It is both scary and exhilarating, but if we want our lives to be renewed, we really have no other choice. Identify the doors. Spend these weeks locating the key(s). You know how to do the rest. (NOTE: If it is a particularly difficult door, ask for someone's help. We never have to do this work all by ourselves.)

A human being who has not a single hour for his/her own every day is not much of a human being.

— RABBI MOSHE LEIB OF SASOV

•

Judaism is a religious path that elevates community and doing for others to the realm of *mitzvah*/commandment. We have always prayed as a group (minyan), using the plural "we" in almost all of our blessings. A full half of the 613 commandments deal with the relationship between one person and another (*mitzvot bein adam l'chavero*). It is difficult, if not impossible, to live a full Jewish life and be a hermit. Even our religious leaders throughout the ages— priests, prophets, and rabbis—were enjoined to marry, raise a family, and work at an occupation.

Perhaps, then, Reb Moshe Leib is speaking to us as a corrective or balance to this focus on others. We need time for ourselves. Time to reflect. Time to think. Time to take a walk, or read a book, or listen to the silence. In my hectic life (we are six people and a dog in my house) serving others, maintaining a home which is often a meeting place for friends, congregants, and strangers, I wake up at 5:00 A.M. so that I can have some alone time. Most days I do this—write. And then I exercise. When I write or work out, I am really doing something for me. Both activities demand my total concentration. Both help me to clarify my thoughts and feelings. Both help me to feel like a human being.

What do you do for yourself each day? What would you like to be doing?

God does not die on the day when we cease to believe in a personal deity, but we die on the day when our lives cease to be illuminated by the steady radiance, renewed daily, of a wonder, the source of which is beyond reason.

— DAG HAMMARSKJÖLD

The "G word" has become difficult for many in our generation. After all, wasn't God supposed to be dead? Or at least less popular than the Beatles? But we see—the signs are all around us—that God is making a comeback. And I believe one of the reasons for this is that many of us have come to recognize that there needs to be a something beyond all our creations, beyond all our selves, in order for life to make sense. I feel comfortable using the "G word," but if that has too much baggage for you, then try the term "Transcendent."

Each day we need to renew this relationship. Is it that ephemeral that it would cease to exist if we neglected it for a day? Is God that insecure? No, it is we who die, a little bit at a time, when we fail to take note of the wonder that is life. And since no day is any less a wonder than any other, this is something we need to do each day. This is probably why you are doing this workout.

Close your eyes, but not too tightly. Feel the radiance of God's light shining on your face. That light is there all the time. All you have to do is close your eyes.

I know that God loves beauty, for the Almighty allows it to flourish everywhere, even in unexpected places.

— BEN ZION BOKSER

I have always loved walking along the ocean, listening to its sound, feeling its breeze, especially during the winter, when few people are around. I always feel so small, and yet at the same time, standing at the ocean's edge, my life seems to make sense. I feel that somehow I fit into the larger picture that is life itself. "We are like the waves," I would think. "For a moment we stand up and are noticed, and then we disappear and become part of the whole. Forever . . ."

But we do not disappear. Not really. We are part of that ocean, perhaps the substance of yet another wave. And even when we die, and our physical presence is no longer seen, we remain part of a much vaster whole which is eternal. All of our lives are like the waves, ever ebbing, ever flowing. Each day we are born anew. Each day we die again.

You were born today. And tonight you will die. What will you do with this time that has been granted?

Blessed are You, Adonai our God, Ruler of the Universe, creating light and creating darkness, making things whole, creating everything.

— Morning prayer

We are accustomed to seeing this prayer translated using the past tense—"who created"—or a noun, "Creator." But the Hebrew voices it in the present, as an active verb, as an ongoing process. In the Hebrew, God is envisioned as a very busy person, each day renewing the work of creation. The world was not born in a single moment, once and forever. It is being created on a daily basis.

And so it is with us as well. Our birth was only the beginning. Each day can be seen as a birthday, at least as a rebirth day. For each day we are new, not held back or determined by anything that occurred the day before.

If you are able, curl up into a fetal position. As you stretch your arms and legs, meditate on how it would feel to be born brand-new this day.

And from there you will seek Adonai your God and find from "there" means from wherever you may happen to be.

— Ba'al Shem Tor

We might think that rebirth or self-renewal is about garnering from the past and/or gearing up for the future. Actually, it is neither of these. In fact, the past and the future are more apt to be barriers, to get in the way of our hope that we can actually be reborn and start anew. For so many of us, the past weighs us down and the future is loaded with expectations, preventing us from any significant movement in our lives.

But as the days continue to get longer and nature is stirring itself back to life, so do we have this moment to look inside ourselves to see that the seeds of renewal are already there. All we have to do is shed some light on them, sprinkle them with life-giving water, plant them in soil that is rich in nutrients, and then nurture them to full growth. This is the promise that spring holds forth for us each and every year.

In Israel right now, the almond trees are getting ready to blossom. Imagine the dead branches of these trees sprouting forth with white flowers. Imagine yourself as one of those branches.

Tu b'Shevat

On the Hebrew calendar, the 15th day of the month of Shevat (Tu b'Shevat) is designated as the day to celebrate the New Year of the Trees. As I was growing up in New York City, it always seemed a bit strange that our rabbis had chosen a midwinter day to celebrate the rebirth of trees. Outside, it was cold and gray, the ground covered in snow, the trees barren of all life. It was not until I lived my first full year in Israel that I saw the almond blossoms appear on the trees right around this time of year. Life was returning. Winter, indeed, was coming to an end. The hope we had expressed in winter's darkest days was (literally) blossoming. It was a cause to celebrate.

meditations
Nature/Environment

One incredible chain of love, of giving, of receiving, unites all of creation; nothing exists singularly by or for itself, but everything is born into an ongoing reciprocal state of action.
— Rabbi Samson Raphael Hirsch

Sometimes it takes a flower to remind us that we are all interconnected, all part of one another. Past, present, and future . . . all that was and all that will ever be. And what a great reminder flowers are—soft, intricate, and ephemeral, each petal seemingly separate but really part of a pattern and a design. They appear, seemingly out of nowhere, take our breath away, color our lives, and then are gone. Like us. Like all of life.

Buy some flowers this week. Examine each one. Gently stroke the petals. Breathe in their fragrance. Thank God for creating such miraculous beauty.

When God created the first human beings, the Lord led them around the Garden of Eden and said, "Look at My works! See how beautiful they are—how excellent! I created them for your sake. See to it that you do not spoil and destroy My world—for if you do, there will be no one else to repair it."

— MIDRASH ECCLESIASTES RABBAH 7:28

We often think that we are the first generation to become environmentally conscious. But here we see that the awareness that we are the earth's caretakers is quite ancient. Though created for our sake, the world does not belong to us. It is God's. We have it on loan. And it is up to us to pass it down, unspoiled and intact, to the next generation. That is our task. Part of what makes us human. We have the power and the responsibility to take proper care of our garden.

And yet we see all around us that we have violated God's command. Our planet has not been destroyed, but it is damaged and hurting. And in the process, we are losing our humanity.

We focus on this issue at this time because subtly, quietly, the earth is beginning to wake from its winter sleep. Though (in most places) we cannot see it, life is returning, sap is flowing inside the trees, buds are forming on their branches, seeds are stirring in the ground, as we move inevitably toward spring. We have celebrated this return with *Tu b'Shevat*, the day designated as the New Year of the Trees. Now it is time to renew our dedication to be planetary caretakers.

What are you personally doing to help maintain our environment? Recycling? Carpooling? Using "safe" products? Contributing to environmental causes? Writing to your legislators? Participating in cleanups? We are the repair persons, the fixers. There is no one else but you.

> *One who buys a tree from a friend for felling shall leave the height of a handbreath from the ground, and then cut it, so that a stump remains from which a new tree can grow.*
>   — TALMUD, BABA BATRA 80B

Who owns the tree that we bought from a friend? Our rabbis seem to indicate that it is not us, that all we get is use of the tree, which must be preserved and passed down to the next generation. It is like the story that is told of the Roman emperor who comes upon an old man in ancient Israel planting a carob tree. "Old man," the emperor says with a laugh, "don't you realize that you will be long dead before this tree ever bears fruit?" "Of course," the old man replies. "I am not planting this tree for myself. But just as my grandparents planted for me, so must I plant for my grandchildren."

We do not own the land, or anything on it. We borrow it from our grandchildren to use, to take care of, and to pass along. God is the ultimate owner. We are renters. And we must make sure it will be there for the next generation.

What is it that you are leaving for the next generation? The one after that?

> *Even those creatures you deem superfluous in this world — like flies, bugs, and gnats — nevertheless have their allotted task in the scheme of creation, as it says, "God looked over everything that had been made and found it very good."*
>   — MIDRASH GENESIS RABBAH 10:7

It all depends on one's perspective. From God's point of view, everything has meaning and purpose, everything is part of a Divine plan. From our point of view, we fail to see as useful anything that does not accrue direct benefit to ourselves. Our challenge is to be more God-like, to get beyond ourselves, to understand our limits, and to begin to appreciate the entirety of this creation. Even those things that we call disasters, like earthquakes, forest fires, volcanoes, and hurricanes, are part of a delicate balance of nature, all necessary for the continued survival of the planet as a whole. Again, we may fail to see that, especially as our homes and property are destroyed or, God forbid, loved ones are lost, but in the big picture, these are all part of the health and vitality of our world.

Think of something that you have failed to appreciate. Think of the positive contribution it is making to your life, and the life of our environment. (NOTE: This is an exercise you can do with people whom you have failed to appreciate as well.)

It is forbidden to live in a town that does not have a green garden.

— TALMUD, YERUSHALMI, KIDDUSHIN 4:12

There are three things I hear when I read this quote. The first is that our quality of life is affected by living in a place that has plants, flowers, and trees. These are not merely "landscaping"; they are part of what makes life livable. The second is that a town that would not create a garden is inhabited by people with whom we should not live. And the third is that as city dwellers, we need to have reminders of nature and God's creation. We need to come into contact with the natural world each and every day. Once upon a time, we all lived within the natural cycles of time. Our food came from the land we worked, our schedules were shaped by the amount of daylight we received, our activities were influenced by the seasons and the time of the year. Modernity has "freed" us from all of that. We can do whatever we want to whenever and wherever we want to do it. If it is cold, we turn up the heat; if it is dark, we turn on the lights; if it is summer we can fly to where it is winter and when it gets too cold we travel to where it is warm. There is something wonderful about all this, but as usual, there has also been a price to pay. We are out of touch with the natural cycle of the universe. Having a garden is one way to remind us that we are all part of a larger chain of being, all part of a magnificent and beautiful creation.

Go to the nearest garden or park in your town. (If there isn't one, call a mover.) Stand in its center. Imagine/remember what it looks and feels like in each of the four seasons. Get a good picture, with as many details as possible, in your head.

Master of the Universe, may it be my custom to go outdoors each day, among the trees and grasses, among all living things, there to be alone and enter into prayer. There may I express all that is in my heart, talking with the One to whom I belong. And may all the grasses, trees, and plants awake at my coming. Send the power of their life into my prayer, making whole my heart and my speech through the life and spirit of growing things, made whole by the Transcendent Source.

— REBBE NACHMAN OF BRATZLAV
(ADAPTED FROM *GATES OF PRAYER*)

When I think of Rebbe Nachman, images of a gaunt, pale, eighteenth-century Polish Hasid come to mind—not exactly "nature boy." All the more remarkable, then, this prayer.

We think of nature as something entrusted to us, something that we need to take care of, as well we should. But it can be the other way around as well. Nature can be taking care of us, empowering us, giving us its energy so that we can go out and do our work in the world. Go outside, if you can. Invite nature to send you its energy. You can use this prayer or your own words.

~ ~ ~

HESED/LOVINGKINDNESS

*The world stands on three things: on Torah, prayer, and acts of
lovingkindness.*

— PIRKE AVOT 1:2

How many times have we said or sung these words at camp or
synagogue? "*Al shlosha devarim* . . ." More times than I can
count. But what do they mean? For the ancients, there was the
belief that three massive pillars supported the earth—that the earth
literally rested on three columns. The rabbis, in writing these
words, were moving away from the idea of physical support to a
metaphysical one. What qualities or actions sustain the world? they
wondered. What keeps the planet going?

Their response was simple, yet profound—Torah (head), prayer
(heart), and acts of lovingkindness (hands and feet). These three
make up the three major paths to God as understood by Jewish
spirituality. Together, they represent wholeness, a complete human
being. Head spirituality is built on study for the sake of truth and
knowledge. Heart spirituality arises out of our opening ourselves
up to God in all our vulnerability. Hands and feet spirituality
requires us to make our lives an act of dedicated service to others.
Each is a valid path. By personality or proclivity we may find
ourselves drawn to one or another or some combination of the
three. Together, they sustain the world.

As the winter season begins to wind down, God's lovingkindness
is demonstrated by the awakening of life. Animals stir in their
habitation, sap is flowing in the trees, the days are noticeably

longer, little sprouts are beginning to appear in some places. What acts of lovingkindness will you perform today? Each day? Will you stop to talk to the homeless person you pass each day on your way to work? Will you volunteer an hour to help a child read? Will you visit someone who is sick? No act is too small. Each one helps to ensure the survival of the planet. We are sustained by such acts.

The beginning and end of Torah is performing acts of loving-kindness.

— TALMUD, SOTAH 14A

The Torah is the primary record of the Jewish people's encounter with God. It is the story of a relationship that really begins with Abraham and Sarah and continues to the exodus from Egyptian slavery and the wilderness wanderings. While Torah formally ends with our people at the borders of the Land of Promise, the story continues through Joshua, kings and prophets, scribes and scholars, poets and storytellers. It continues with you and me, and with anyone who would live a life of holiness, a life of attempting to do God's will. So long as there is a you and me, the final chapter has not yet been written.

And how do we write this Torah? It is very simple. Through acts of lovingkindness. That is Torah's beginning; that is its end. We are what we do. And the opportunity to demonstrate lovingkindness is never too far from our fingertips. What about today? What act of lovingkindness will you perform? What opportunity to "write a new chapter of Torah" will come your way? Will you seize it, or let it slip away?

Adonai, Adonai, a God of compassion and grace, slow to anger, abounding in lovingkindness, a God of truth, extending loving-kindness to the thousandth generation, forgiving iniquity, transgression, and sin . . .

— EXODUS 34:6

There are two story lines in the tale of Moses. The first, and the one on which we tend to focus, is his leadership of the children of Israel in their forty years of wandering through the wilderness. The second is Moses' ongoing relationship with God, and God's increasing level of self-disclosure to him. At one point, Moses asks, "Let me see Your face" (i.e., full disclosure), and God responds, "You cannot see Me and still be alive . . . what I can do is reveal to you my most intimate attributes."

Among those attributes, numbered at thirteen is *rav hesed*: abounding lovingkindness. God loves us. And God shows that love through acts of lovingkindness. We are the recipients each and every day of this love, though sometimes we forget that or take it for granted. But we ought make remembering part of our daily routine.

What acts of lovingkindness did God shower upon you today? Did you remember to say thanks?

Be the living expression of God's lovingkindness—kindness in your face, kindness in your eyes, kindness in your smile, kindness in your warm greeting.

— MOTHER TERESA

The word *hesed* shares the same Hebrew root as "Hasid." In the eighteenth century, throughout Europe, there developed grassroots religious movements known as Pietism. These movements came about in response to the official expressions of religion, which were seen as both the domain of the wealthy and as overly intellectual and devoid of feeling. In Judaism, the Pietistic movement was known as Hasidism. Led by the innkeeper-become-itinerant-preacher known as the Ba'al Shem Tov, Hasidism was distinguished by its call for joyous fervor in prayer coupled with simple acts of lovingkindness that anyone could perform for his/her neighbor. Its popularity swept through the Jewish communities of northern

Europe, especially the poorest ones in Poland and Russia. Soup kitchens, *bikur cholim*/groups that visited the sick, *chevra kaddisha*/burial societies, as well as a wide variety of other social services, became the hallmark of these early Hasidic dynasties.

More than any other well-known person in our own time, Mother Teresa has embodied the principle of *hesed* in her life's actions. Hers was a life of action on behalf of others, especially the downtrodden and the outcasts of the world. If God showers us with lovingkindness, then we, in imitation of God, need to do the same.

Throughout your day, you will have numerous opportunities to treat others with lovingkindness. What will you do with those opportunities? What did you do with yesterday's?

The highest wisdom is lovingkindness.
— TALMUD, BERACHOT 17A

We tend to think of wisdom as something acquired through study, or age, or the pondering of life's great questions. We think of it as the domain of the elders of society, who seem to know just what to say and what to advise. So why does the Talmud say that lovingkindness is the highest wisdom? What does one have to do with the other?

If wisdom is about the power of discernment and proper judgment, of knowing what is right and true, then at least some of that wisdom ought to go beyond the abstract, extending to the way we treat others. And when we deal with others, we always need to ask ourselves, "How would we like to be treated?" as well as, "How does God want us to treat them?" The answer to both questions is: "With lovingkindness." We know that is the right thing to do. We know how we feel when we are treated that way. And we know that is what God truly wants, even expects of us. To act in accord with God's will, this is the mark of the wise. To make our own will the same as God's, this too, is a sign that we have acquired a heart of wisdom.

What prevents you from being wise (i.e., from treating others with lovingkindness)?

Kindness is always undeserved. And what rejoices one's heart is precisely what s/he is given as a sheer gift.

— RUDOLF BULTMANN

The stance of the religious person is precisely this: I do not "deserve" the lovingkindness that I receive. I am not entitled to it. And when (or if) it comes my way, my only appropriate response is gratitude and a heart filled with joy. This is not to say we are bad or worthless people, or that no one should ever do anything for us because we "don't deserve it." Rather, it is a recognition that everything we do receive is a gift. In other words, our quote this day does not so much characterize us as it characterizes that which we receive.

And we receive so much. Without doing anything, we are showered with lovingkindness each and every day. This is not to say that our lives are perfect or even problem-free. We are all wounded, and each of us has known suffering and pain. But the quote is meant to focus our attention on the part of our cup that is at least half full. Imagine your life as that half-filled cup. All that fills it are gifts. Take a good look at those gifts. I hope they fill your heart with cause to rejoice.

＊ ＊ ＊

m e d i t a t i o n s
HAPPINESS

As the month of Adar enters, one should increase in happiness.
— TALMUD, TA'ANIT 29A

The month of Adar precedes Passover. (In Jewish leap years, which occur seven times every nineteen years, there are two months of Adar.) Passover, as understood by the Torah, is the beginning of the year; it, rather than what we know as "Rosh Hashanah," is called the first month. On the historical level (linear time), Passover, which celebrates the exodus from Egypt, represents the birth of the Jewish people. On the cosmic level (cyclical time), Passover, which inaugurates spring, represents the (re)birth of all life. No matter how one counts time, Passover is a new beginning.

A month before Passover, then, recognizing that we did not die, that winter did not kill us or the planet, we are told to be happy. For this is the beginning, the core of happiness. A recognition that we are alive. That's it. Later this month, you will have the hard work of getting ready for Passover. But not now.

So when is the last time you were happy, really happy, just for being alive? It's Adar. Be happy.

If you are not happy without the long list of your desires, then getting what you want will not bring you happiness.
— RABBI ABRAHAM TWERSKI

Where does happiness come from? Most of us approach it as if it comes from outside of ourselves. Getting something we have wanted, accomplishing some task, meeting the right person, finding the right job . . . these are supposed to be the sources of our happiness. But they are not. And the happiness they bring is very short-lived. They fill us up for a little while and then we are on to our next quest. We deceive ourselves by thinking we can find happiness out there in the external world, when all along the only place to look is inside ourselves.

Despite living in an era of unprecedented affluence, with the ability to go anywhere and have anything, we still do not know how to be happy. Can it be that we are looking in the wrong place? Where are you seeking happiness? Are you finding it there? If not, are you willing to turn your gaze inward?

To find happiness in what one has to do, not simply in what one wants to do, this is a blessing of God.

— GOETHE

It is easy to be happy when we are doing what we want. After all, it is our choice. No one asked us to do it; we want to. But to be happy doing that which we have to be doing . . . that is a greater challenge. On some level, we need to recognize that even the things we have to do are choices. It may not always seem that way, especially when the task is unpleasant, but very rarely are we forced to do anything. We are there to fulfill some unspoken or uncon- scious need, to uphold an image of ourselves, even to avoid feeling guilty. We do not like to acknowledge or admit that, but it is most often true. We are making choices all the time.

Nevertheless, there are things we have to do. In fact, most of us spend most of our lives doing things we have to do, whether or not we are choosing them. We go to work, clean our houses, do the laundry, get dinner on the table, wash the dishes, drive children to and from their activities, take care of aging parents, wake in the middle of the night to comfort a crying child or change a diaper, pay our bills, attend boring meetings and fulfill social obligations. Did I leave anything out? If we do not find a measure of happiness in doing these tasks, then most of our lives will be unhappy.

Think of one thing you do that you have to do that you would prefer not doing. Now you have a choice. You can be miserable, cursing your lot in life, or you can feel a sense of pride or accomplishment, even happiness that you are able to scratch it off your list for today. You choose.

Happy are the ones who dwell in Your house . . . happy is the people whose God is Adonai.

— DAILY LITURGY

Sitting in God's house is a metaphor for aligning ourselves with God's purpose, for living a life in consonance with the One. It does not mean that we are always right, or that life will be easy and free of trouble. But it does mean we will always know where we are and to whom we belong. It means we will always know where home is and our place in it.

Who is your God? I mean your real God, not the one to whom you pay lip service. Whom do you serve? Whose will is more important than your own? What voice commands you in your day-to-day existence? What is more important to you than anything else? That is your God. Do you spell it, "A-d-o-n-a-i?" There is no true happiness unless you do.

A Nazarite is considered a sinner . . . This is so because he afflicted himself by voluntarily and needlessly abstaining from wine. If a person who abstained only from wine is called a sinner, how much the more so is the person who ascetically refrains from all enjoyment.

— TALMUD, BABA KAMA 91B

Judaism is not a path for hedonists or ascetics. It is not a path for those who just want to "go for it," no matter what the consequences. Neither is it a path for those who would like to live the hermit's life on top of the mountain. It is a middle path that asks us to become involved in the world without getting overly absorbed by it. It is a path of moderation that wants us to enjoy life while controlling our appetites and sanctifying the everyday to God, making everything holy. Judaism wants us to enjoy life and to be happy.

Are you deriving pleasure from your day-to-day activities? If so, good for you; it is a Jewish thing to do. If not, why not? How can you make sure to do those things that will bring some happiness into your life?

And Mordechai sent letters to all the Jews to keep the fourteenth and fifteenth of the month of Adar as days in which our people rested from their enemies, and the month which for them turned sorrow into happiness, a day of mourning into a holiday, days of feasting and joy, of sending food to one another, and gifts to the poor.

— ESTHER 9:21–2

I think if you asked the average person what s/he wants out of life, the response would almost always be, "All I want is to be happy." And people do want happiness, not only for themselves but for their children as well. We work hard at making ourselves happy. We buy books and attend classes, change our diets and our lifestyles, build new homes or remodel old ones, all in an attempt to find that elusive quality called happiness.

To be happy is to be delighted, pleased, or glad; it is a mood of joy, felicity, or contentment. To be happy is to feel undisturbed, untroubled, safe. As Americans, in our very Constitution, we are guaranteed the right to the pursuit of happiness. And I am sure each of us has known moments of such happiness—at least I hope we have. But like most emotions, happiness is elusive and ephemeral; it comes and goes and is really beyond our control. A continual state of happiness is not only unobtainable, it is not something we really need. I would even go so far as to say that given the realities of our world today, in light of all the pain and suffering that exist, to be happy all the time would be a scandal, would be a life not worth living.

But this (Purim, the month of Adar) is a moment of happiness. We have escaped our enemies, overcome winter and death. As Jews, we share it with others and remember those less fortunate than ourselves—in this case, the poor and the needy. How will you share your happiness? What will you do today to help make someone else happy?

❧   ❧   ❧

meditations
Evil/Dealing with Enemies

Evil, then, is that force, residing inside or outside human beings, that seeks to kill life or liveliness.

— M. Scott Peck

In modern times, we have been taught that there is no such thing as evil, that with proper social engineering, the elimination of poverty, and a quality education for everyone, we could eliminate what was once termed "evil" by the Bible and religions. The twentieth century has exposed that notion as idealistic folly, yet many of us continue to hold on to it. The human capacity to do evil has not been diminished; it persists among the well educated as well as the wealthy. Being poor and illiterate are no prerequisites to hurting another human being, an animal, or our environment. In fact, we often find the opposite to be the case—the greatest compassion and kindness are found among those who have the least.

Evil is part of our world, part of our human nature. Each of us, under the right circumstances, has the capacity to commit evil. Evil occurs throughout our world, and though we might not want to call it such, we read about it in our newspapers each and every day.

Where is the evil in you? What evil have you done? What are the forces that keep it in check?

Hate evil, love good.

—AMOS 5:15

Love good. That is the easy part. We all want to show our love for that which is good in this world. Goodness is a sustaining force, one of those things that makes life worth living. We want to surround ourselves with goodness. And loving something helps to bring it close.

But hate evil? How can a religion tell us to hate anything? Isn't hate the antithesis of what religion is all about? However, if love is what brings something close, then perhaps hate can push it farther away. And when it comes to evil, our tradition wants us to distance ourselves, to get as far away from it as possible. You see, one of the mistakes we sometimes make concerning evil is to accommodate it. Wanting to be good people, we try to show kindness and compassion to all living things, especially other human beings. Our hearts do not allow us to believe that evil is real, that there are evil people in this world. We want to believe that people are basically good, and that if we cannot see this quality in another, it is our shortcoming.

So, if you had the opportunity, would you destroy evil? Can you hate it? Hating evil is a spiritual challenge that enables us to see the world, and others, as they truly are, not how we want them to be. Try visualizing that which you consider to be evil, and imagine physically distancing yourself from it—actually taking steps away. By hating it, those steps will be easier to take.

They [the rabbis] balanced their belief in people's ineradicable potential to turn from evil and do good with the tough-minded understanding that people are very much more the creatures of their will-to-do-evil, their yetzer ha-ra, rather than their will-to-do-good, their yetzer ha-tov.

— RABBI EUGENE BOROWITZ

We are, each of us, a battleground. Forces rage within us, competing against one another for our hearts and minds, as well as for our actions. These forces have been described differently by philosophers, theologians, psychologists, and others, but I think we all realize that a human being is much more than merely a creature of instinct and habit. We think, we struggle, we change our minds, we want to do certain things and then feel we shouldn't, or we do them and then feel bad about ourselves. The rabbis called these forces *yetzer ha-ra* and *yetzer ha-tov*: the will-to-do-evil and the will-to-do-good. But even these forces were complex and multifaceted. For the rabbis said that without *yetzer ha-ra,* no one would marry, have children, build a home, or establish a career. Clearly, *yetzer ha-ra* also has something to do with self-preservation and ego strength, both necessary for our health and survival.

But if that is all we are, concerned only with our self-preservation and survival, then truly we are evil. For our love and care of others, our protection of the world and its environment, our concern for future generations—these lift our humanity, this is what makes us fully human. The rabbis felt that the *yetzer ha-ra* had the upper hand and therefore had to be held in check through great effort on our parts. They understood that in this struggle we would fail as often as we succeeded. Nevertheless, they enjoined us to do battle every moment of every day, for the full measure of our humanity rests in our ability to restrain our desire to do evil.

How goes the battle within you?

Remember what Amalek did to you on your journey out of Egypt . . . Therefore, when Adonai your God has given you rest from all your enemies that surround you in the Land of Promise, you shall erase the memory of Amalek from under heaven. Don't forget!

— DEUTERONOMY 25:17,19

Remember to forget! Isn't that a curious commandment— paradoxical, impossible? Why, then, does Torah ask it of us? What is the motivation?

The root of evil, our Torah teaches us, is found in the people known as the Amalekites. King Saul had the opportunity to destroy them totally, but in his compassion, he spared their leader (King Agag) and their female children. Years later, an Agagite known as Haman attempted state-sponsored genocide against our people. In every generation, there seems to be some Haman or other who would do the same. Our challenge, then as now, is to recognize the evil that exists in the world and wipe it out, wipe out even the memory of it. This is not about vengeance, as it is commonly misunderstood. It is not about a lack of compassion or forgiveness. It is about eliminating evil from our midst. There can be no messianic time, no era of peace while evil continues to hold sway.

Are you ready to be a warrior against evil?

Evil talk is so grievous a sin because it kills three people: the one who speaks evil, the one who listens to it, and the one about whom it is spoken.

— TALMUD, ERACHIN 15B

I have never met a person who considers him/herself evil, yet we go about our day gossiping about others. Gossip, called *lashon ha-ra* in Hebrew, is "evil talk." And if the Talmud is right about this, then when we gossip, we are guilty of murder.

When we are confronted with this fact, most of us say, "But what I said was true." The fact that it was "true" makes it gossip. If it was not true, then it is slander. Gossiping about others alters our relationship with them. It changes the relationship between the one to whom we have spoken and the one about whom we have spoken. And it changes the way people think about us. They have to wonder when it will be their turn to be the subjects of our gossip. This change in relationship is like a death, because it limits the full potential of our interaction with others.

If we do not talk about others, what else is there to talk about? We can begin with ourselves. Imagine if you were limited to that in every conversation if you could only talk about yourself—your thoughts, your experiences, your feelings. And what if your partner were "limited" in the same way. Imagine how this would deepen the level of exchange between you. Try it. Try it for a day. See if you can spend even one day without gossiping.

It is better to be called a fool all my life, rather than be wicked for a single moment before God.

— MISHNA, EDUYOT 5:6

I think one contributing factor to our willingness to commit evil, big acts as well as small, lies in the assumption or feeling that no one is watching. "What difference does it make?" we think. "Everyone is doing it, and getting away with it. Why should I be any different?" But imagine for a second that we really believed in a God who was omniscient and omnipresent, in a God who sees and knows all. Imagine if our lives were being recorded and if we each had to make a reckoning before the Holy One. I would like to think it would make a big difference. We would still fail, because we are human and imperfect. But our rush to do evil, I believe, would be radically curtailed. We would even rather be made to look foolish than to appear wicked before the Lord, our God.

Most of us are good people. Yet even good people do evil. Especially pernicious are the little acts of evil we do not even notice. Take note of them today. Watch yourself do them. And then ask yourself, "Is this the way I want to appear before God?"

AFTERWORD
THE CYBER MINYAN

❧

And what is the proof that the Shechina is present when ten peo-ple pray together? "Elohim stands in the congregation of God."
— TALMUD, BERACHOT 6A

Minyan is a very powerful idea. It creates community, it keeps us regular in our prayer discipline (i.e., we are more likely to show up if someone is "counting" on us), and it provides a space in which we can connect to God and self. Until the advent of modernity, the minyan occupied a central place in the lives of Jewish men. Whether it was peer pressure, the *halachic*/legal system which required it, or the inner need to express one's spiritual longings, showing up at the synagogue (and there were small synagogues everywhere) was a regular feature in one's day. Since women were "released" from all time-bound commandments and thereby not required to pray, they generally did not become part of these prayer circles, nor would they count in the minyan. This is still the case in all orthodox and some conservative synagogues. Women's need for prayer was met privately, if at all, though there are legends of individual women who regularly prayed in the back of the synagogue.

Once upon a time—and not so very long ago—we all lived in community, real community. There was Baltimore's Forest Park and later Pikesville with its Park Heights Avenue; 105th Street and then Shaker Heights in Cleveland. There was Delmar Boulevard in St. Louis's University City. Milwaukee had its West Side. There were the Grand Concourse in the Bronx and Eastern Parkway in my own native Brooklyn. But community was not just geographical. It was a social mentality—the knowledge that you belonged there, that these were your people, that their story was yours. You went to the same clubs, your children went to the same schools and, for the most part, married one another and settled down in the same neighborhood. All that has changed. Think about it. How many of you live in the same neighborhood in which you grew up? How many of your friends or acquaintances do? If you are like me, I am sure it is a very small percentage.

Modernity broke down the idea of community and, by discounting the spiritual as "outmoded" or "medieval," suppressed the need in us all. We were to find our fulfillment as individuals, through our own accomplishments in school and work. The family and the company would replace the community, and marriage would become the central relationship of our lives. No longer would we live our lives in one place; instead, we would go wherever there was an opportunity for us to "better" our lives. It should not be surprising that we are suffering.

While we may no longer have the type of lifestyle or live in the kind of community that allow for us to be a part of a daily minyan, we are rediscovering our needs in these realms of life. Because we have accomplished all that we were told would bring us happiness and still find it wanting, the need for spirituality and community have reemerged in our time. While some of us may be able to reconstitute our lives so that we may live in self-contained communities, most of us will not. We want to connect with our spiritual resources, and we want to connect with others, but we will have to do so in a way that fits our life pattern and our present-day realities. In addition, in a world that is increasingly interdependent, and in which global communication is instantaneous, our idea of community is undergoing change. Why not, then, a cyber minyan? For right now, it may be the best we can do.

A cyber minyan is one in which we recognize that others are doing the same thing we are—opening ourselves to the Transcendent, saying the same words and blessings—but doing so in different places, perhaps even at the same time. It may not satisfy all our needs for community; in fact I am sure it will not. But it may help us overcome some of the loneliness and isolation we feel. And it may also add to our growing notion of a global community, all descendants of the One.

APPENDIX

~

Additional prayers and blessings that you can fit into your workout on a regular basis or as the situation warrants. Several of these original versions of traditional prayers have been set to music by Cantor Rachelle Nelson, and are available on the CD, "Bless Our Days."

FOR GRATITUDE

If our mouths were filled with song
As the waters fill the sea
And our tongues rang out in joy
As the roaring of the waves;
If our lips offered praise
As the heaven's wide expanse
And our eyes were to shine
As brightly as the sun;
If our arms opened wide
like an eagle in the sky
And our feet were as swift
As a deer running free;
Still we could not thank You
Lord, our God
Or bless Your name enough
For Your kindness to us all.

Modim anachnu Lach
You are our God, Rock of our life;
Modim anachnu Lach

You are our God, Shield of salvation;
Forever and ever
Morning, noon, and night.
Modim anachnu Lach
We sing Your praises
Modim anachnu Lach
Compassionate One, Merciful Lord;
Forever and ever
Morning, noon, and night
Modim anachnu Lach
Our lives are in Your hands
Our souls are in Your keeping
Your miracles surround us day by day.
Our lives are in Your hands,
Our souls are in Your keeping,
Your never-ending love has always been our hope.
We will never stop praising Your name.

FOR CLARITY OF PURPOSE
(can be used as a mantra)

Show me Your way
That I may do Your will;
Show me my path
That I may walk in peace.
Ga'lay lee dar'key
V'eh ha'laych b'shalom;
R'ay lee cha'fetz'cha
V'eh'ha'laych b'shalom.

AWARENESS OF THE MIRACLES OF DAILY LIVING

Baruch Atah Adonai Eloheinu, Melech haOlam, asher natan
la'sech'vee vee'na, l'hav'cheen bain yome oo'vain laye'lah;
Blessed are You, Adonai our God, for bestowing the ability to
distinguish between day and night.

Baruch Atah Adonai Eloheinu, Melech haOlam, sheh'ah'sah'nee
b'tzal'mo;
. . . for creating me in Your image.

Baruch Atah Adonai Eloheinu, Melech haOlam, sheh'ah'sah nee
ben/bat cho'reen;
. . . for giving me freedom.

Baruch Atah Adonai Eloheinu, Melech haOlam, sheh'ah'sha'nee
Yis'rah'ale;
. . . for making me a Jew.

Baruch Atah Adonai Eloheinu, Melech haOlam, po'kay'ach
eev'reem;
. . . for giving us the capacity to see.

Baruch Atah Adonai Eloheinu, Melech haOlam, mal'beesh
ah'roo'meem;
. . . for providing the materials to make clothes.

Baruch Atah Adonai Eloheinu, Melech haOlam, mah'teer
ah'soo'reem;
. . . for the ability to stretch our bodies.

Baruch Atah Adonai Eloheinu, Melech haOlam, zo'kafe k'foo'feem;
. . . for straightening our backs.

Baruch Atah Adonai Eloheinu, Melech haOlam, sheh'ah'sah'lee kole
tzar'kee;
. . . for providing for my daily needs.

Baruch Atah Adonai Eloheinu, Melech haOlam, ha'may'cheen
meetz'ah'day gah'vair;
. . . for giving us guidance along life's path/allowing me to walk.

Baruch Atah Adonai Eloheinu, Melech haOlam, oh'zair Yis'rah'ale
  beeg'voo'rah;
. . . for endowing our people with courage.
Baruch Atah Adonai Eloheinu, Melech haOlam, oh'tair Yis'rah'ale
  b'teef'ah'rah;
. . . for crowning our people with glory.
Baruch Atah Adonai Eloheinu, Melech haOlam, ha'no'tain
  la'yah'afe ko'ach;
. . . for giving strength to the weary.
Baruch Atah Adonai Eloheinu, Melech haOlam, ha'mah'ah'veer
  shay'nah may'ay'naye oot'noo'mah may'af'ah'pai;
. . . for energizing me for a new day.

FOR PRAISING GOD
(can be used as a mantra)

B'chol yom ah'vahr'cheh'cha
vah'ah'hah'l'lah sheem'cha l'oh'lahm vah'ed
Every day I will bless You
And praise Your name, forever and ever.   (Psalm 145:2)

BLESSING FOR THE MONTH AHEAD

May it be Your will
Adonai our God
God of our mothers
God of our fathers
to renew our lives
in the coming month.

Chaim shel shalom
toe'vah oo'vrah'cha

Grant us
long life, a peaceful life

a life of goodness and blessing
radiance and health;
a life of abundance and honor
dignity and strength;
a life free of shame and reproach
evil and sin
embracing heaven
with love of Torah;
a life of joy and happiness
comfort and deliverance
our hearts' desires fulfilled
fulfilled only for good.

Free us from our exile
our exile from one another

For this we pray
Amen, *seh'lah.*

FOR WORLD PEACE

Sha'lome rahv ahl Yis'rah'ale ahm'cha, ahm'cha
Ta'seem l'oh'lahm, ta'seem l'oh'lahm
Key Ah'tah who Meh'lech l'chol ha'sha'lome
V'tove b'ay'neh'cha l'vah'rech et ahm'cha Yis'rah'ale
B'chol'ate, oo'v'chol sha'ah beesh'low'meh'cha

Bring peace, bring peace
To Your people
Yis'rah'ale

For You are the One, *Ah'done l'chol ha'sha'lome*
V'tove b'ay'neh'cha bless Your people *Yis'rah'ale*
Every moment, every day *beesh'lo'meh'cha*

Ba'ruch Ah'tah Adonai, bless Your people, *Yis'rah'ale,* with peace,
 ba'sha'lome.

About the Author

Rabbi Bookman is available for a limited number of workshops, lectures and presentations. Many of the blessings and prayers in this book are available on a recording by Cantor Rachelle Nelson, entitled *Bless Our Days*. You can contact him or order CDs, tapes, songbooks and sheet music (including a cassette version of The Workout) by calling *In the Spirit Music* at 1-877-SOUL WORK. You can also write to the Rabbi at his E-mail address rebbeaid@aol.com.